The Next Chapter

by Beryl McClary

13th & Joan Publishing House

Beryl McClary is beautiful inside and out and this book reflects her transferring that same beauty into the world. Her loving spirit and words are infectious.

– **Marie Benjamin, Attorney**

Beryl McClary is the type of person that makes you a better person just by association with her. She is kind, insightful, and committed to excellence and the book demonstrates her spirit-filled mission and determination to help all middle-aged women reach their full potential.

– **Lajuana Miller, The Links Incorporated**

Beryl is a heartfelt and cheerful friend that is always willing to listen. Every part of this book inspires and allows you to arrive at your own conclusions while thinking about the story of your life and the next chapter that you will write.

– **Deborah Jones, Friend**

I've known Beryl for many years. She continues to be an energetic forward moving woman firmly rooted in God's word and the 21st century. It was an honor to read about her next chapters but to also be inspired to make decisions about my own.

– **Rosalyn Bonds Greene, Attorney**

The Next Chapter

by Beryl McClary

13th & Joan Publishing House

The Next Chapter. Copyright 2020 by Beryl McClary. All rights reserved. No part of this publication may be reproduced, distributed, or transmitted in any form or by any means, including photocopying, recording, or other electronic or mechanical methods, without the prior written permission of the publisher, except in the case of brief quotations embodied in critical reviews and certain other noncommercial uses permitted by copyright law.

For permission requests, write to the publisher, addressed "Attention: Permissions Coordinator," 500 N. Michigan Avenue, Suite #600, Chicago, IL 60611. 13th & Joan books may be purchased for educational, business or sales promotional use. For information, please email the Sales Department at sales@13thandjoan.com.

Printed in the U. S. A.

First Printing, August 2020

Library of Congress Cataloging-in-Publication Data has been applied for.

ISBN: 978-1-7342346-6-4

Epigraph

"I trust the next chapter because I am holding the pen."

– Beryl McClary

Contents

Acknowledgments i
Preface iii
Introduction v
Prologue vii

Section 1: MIND

CHAPTER 1
SELF-PERCEPTION 1

CHAPTER 2
MENTAL HEALTH 7

CHAPTER 3
PERCEPTION OF THE WORLD 11

CHAPTER 4
STAYING SHARP 17

CHAPTER 5
TECH 21

Section 2: BODY

CHAPTER 6
EXERCISE 31

CHAPTER 7
NUTRITION 37

CHAPTER 8
FASHION 43

CHAPTER 9
RECHARGING 49

Section 3: SOUL

CHAPTER 10 SPIRITUALITY	59
14 Days of Self-Reflection	64
CHAPTER 11 RELATIONSHIPS	73
CHAPTER 12 TRAVEL	81
CHAPTER 13 MONEY	85
CHAPTER 14 DISCOVERING PURPOSE	89
EPILOGUE	94
Closing Sentiments	95
ABOUT THE AUTHOR	99

Acknowledgments

Like most things in my life, this book would not have been possible without the close-knit, Heaven-sent people around me who encouraged me to finish when I was close to giving up.

To my dear husband, Thomas McClary. I love you so much, and being married to you has been nothing short of a fairytale. Thank you for embracing my dream and loving me through this process. After so many years of marriage, we still have much more left in our journey. I couldn't thank God enough for allowing me to embark on it with you.

Then to my children Jazmyne, Ashley, Ryan, Brandon, Maya and Mariah — my own personal cheerleading squad that never had a lack of energy or opinions. And to my youngest son, Gabriel. You were the in-house editor I didn't know I needed. You worked with me to write the best sentences I could and tell the story I wanted to tell. And sometimes parents can forget to tell their children thank you, so I'm doing that here: Thank you, Gabey Baby! All my children, regardless of biology, have been a blessing to me. You are all my reason for what I do.

My sisters Priscilla, who always told me everything would come out alright, Viviloria, always there to help, and always reminded me to see the bright side of things, and Lutricia Sowell who would always remind me to be nice. Lutricia and Priscilla, there is not a day that goes by that I do not think of you. It seems like yesterday I was just a little girl and Priscilla was bossing me around like she was Mother and Lutricia was there to try and keep something that resembled peace. Then there is my younger brother Vasco Thompson III, the loudest and funniest person I know. You keep me in fighting shape and I never get tired of your playful teasing and tumultuous humor.

To my Dad, Vasco Thompson , Jr., who would always find a way to help get me to where I needed to be, no matter what. With time, I realize how much you sacrificed for me and my siblings growing up, and you gave us a fair chance at life, all without complaining one time.

To Ardre Orie, my publisher, I am forever so grateful for your insight and wisdom. Thank you for your excellence and patience as you championed this mother and lawyer to own her story and share it with the world.

Then to my friends that have been with me since elementary school, who now seem like family, Carolyn Gail Lindsey, the queen of understanding and encouragement. We laughed so much during the years that I'm sure we've added a few extra years to our lives. Debbie Jones, my sweet sister and exercise partner from afar. One day, we'll stop complaining about everything that has to do with the gym. I'm not sure when exactly that day is coming though. Lastly, Margaret McCalman. Where do I even begin? On paper it says "assistant" but you are truly much, much more than that. We are connected at the soul and I can't imagine where I'd be without you. You were the flame that sparked me to write this book. You saw my potential before I even did. And I can't express how grateful I am to have you in my life.

It's impossible for me to list, and express my gratitude for, everyone who makes up my village. So thank you to everyone who has taken me along their journeys to their next chapters, as I have taken you along for mine.

Preface

Calligraphy

I dare you to pick up a pen and write a new story in the book of your life.

-Beryl McClary-

Would you believe me if I told you that I have been composing this book for my entire life? The truth is that you too have been writing the chapters of your story since the day you made your grand entrance into the world. And whether you know it or not, the story of your life and the chapters filled with your existence are invaluable. The way that you dare to use your story is what determines whether or not you recognize how important it is.

Over the years, I began to categorize the series of events that manifested in my life, and I recognized that they were not a result of coincidence or occuring by mistake. Life was unfolding right before my eyes to teach me a series of crucial lessons about how to thrive and not just survive. Today, I recognize more than ever that life has been my greatest teacher. Far too often, we search aimlessly for advice and sentiments from strangers in hopes of discovering anything that can change the direction of our lives, empower us to achieve our goals set, and inspire us to beat the odds. And even after we find said individuals and consume whatever it is that they are selling, we are still left unfulfilled. The problem is that we didn't seek our individual stories for answers first. I repeat, your story is your greatest teacher. About three years prior, I made the conscious decision to write this book and share this discovery. This book became my effort to tell the world that God is the ultimate author and illustrator of our stories, and that paying attention to how he shapes, orchestrates and articulates our lives is the most profound source of information that we search for relentlessly.

The closer I began to pay attention, the more I recognized that God captivates our attention by giving us details, events and plot twists that we didn't see coming.

Writing this book has proven to be a self-enlightening experience as I recalled significant milestones and incidents that shaped the course of my story. This process was not a simple stroll down memory lane, yet a cultivation of a life rooted in service and a quest to channel exceptional power that I knew had been placed inside of me. And while I'd love to say that every day has been sweet, I'd be remiss if I didn't carefully distinguish the times that made me feel as though I was walking on shaky ground. No matter what, every day that I have been blessed to witness was one that God made, and it is in that spirit that I share my footnotes of life with you. If there is one thing that I know for certain, it is that we have the power to leverage every chapter of our stories written in the book of our lives to make ourselves and the world better. It is in this spirit that I share The Next Chapter with you.

Introduction
You Must Do This For You

Don't stop living until you have created a life that you are eager to live.

-**Beryl McClary**-

If you remember nothing else that I have stated thus far, never forget that reading this book is an action that you are taking for you. The contents and the pages of this book have been constructed to encourage you to spend time with yourself in remembrance of what you dare to dream of and how you desire to present yourself to the rest of the world.

And to be brutally honest, I admit that it is possible to sum up the pages of this entire book with one simple sentence. This sentence is a sentiment that emerged as an intense revelation gifted to me in recent years. Today, I recognize it as a universal truth and guiding principle for my life. This level of truth dictates that walking in the realm of possibilities can set you free. It is my hope that you will find yourself amidst the deepest pages of this book but should you decide to soak up the value at this moment, go for it!

The problem with the way that you live is that you believe that you have time. You believe that you will be gifted with time to act out your heart's desires, to love the way you are called to love, to forgive the way that you are called to forgive, and to pursue the goals so big that they wake you in the middle of the night. The truth that no one dares to speak of is that we do not have time. Time is promised to no one. You might be wondering how you can address such a monstrosity of a concept. How then is it possible to live a purposeful life in the absence of the time to do so? The answer is quite simple. We must learn to live every moment of our lives as if there will be no more. As simple as that sounds, I must admit that it has taken me six decades to walk in the fullness of this commitment to the gift of life given unto me. Like everyone else, I have been consumed with the day-to-day race. I too have put off many hopes, dreams and aspirations to serve those whom I love. I too have lived with the regret from not pursuing all of my dreams, while placing them on hold for a later date. From giving of my heart as a loving wife and mother to running my business as an attorney on a mission to be the change I wished to see in the world, I too have been consumed with doing life. In this space, there is no harm no foul but in the fullness of truth, I can admit that there is little room for writing new chapters. We have all been called to give everything that we can humanly offer to the moments that are right in front of us and at times, they are all-consuming. The only fault in living from day to day is not doing the things that our hearts desire because we believe that we must put them off until a later date.

Today, my message and calling is rooted in serving as a beacon of light and a pillar of hope and encouragement that no matter what you aspire to do, you deserve to give yourself the opportunity to take action. You deserve to achieve what your heart desires.

The pages of this book are filled with encouragement for every aspect of your life, which I have categorized in three distinct ways: Mind, Body and Soul. If we seek to illuminate these areas of our lives, then we have access to divine purpose and the abundance of the universe.

In this book, I have laid out my sentiments, short stories and anecdotes that further prove that we have the power to pick up the pen and serve as the co-author of our lives when God holds the pen. The most important factor is that we remember that with every stroke and every new chapter formed, we must never lose sight of the internal motivations, desires and drive to ensure that we remain spiritually full enough to pour into the rest of the world. If you are reading this book, then you have been called for such a time as this to recommit to writing your next chapter. Pick up your pen.

Prologue

To Thine Own Self Be True

The sweltering heat in Leesburg, Florida bore early fruit in winter. My daddy would load the fruit onto the trucks and it would eventually get dumped into bins. You could see the trucks lined up for what seemed like miles, waiting for their turn. Daddy would have me drive him out to the grove like clockwork each year. At times, I would occupy myself by allowing my feet to get stuck in the soft sand. "Beryl, Beryl," Daddy would say. Maybe he wanted me to focus on the real reason we were there, but it was like a field trip for me. The drive was bumpy and I admittedly did a poor job of following the path. To this day, I am still unsure why he would let me drive him. He knew that more than anything, I wanted to be there. I would even go as far as to request that he wake me up so that I could watch the process. The citrus plant mesmerized me and the huge groves in Florida gave me more than enough to see.

Sometimes more than just I would accompany Daddy. My siblings would often go with us. Little did I know this was a babysitting tactic that Momma used when she needed to get to work. We thought very little of the tactic, as we were more concerned with earning our Christmas money. The conversations that sometimes turned into arguments were a surefire sign of the fact that we were siblings.

"You might be old, but you are not my mama," I would say to Pricialla. My older sister was 16 years older than me, and I can remember our exchanges like it was yesterday. I remember when she met a Bahamian man and was preparing to elope. She took me with her to get the rings. The family didn't think very much of him, but I was the one who told my parents about her plans. She was mad at me forever, but she loved me always, and I loved her back.

Viviloria, my second sister, was 15 years older than me. She studied pharmacy at FAMU. She always had a gift for me when she returned home. She was astute and also an activist. "Don't you come from Tallahassee bringing all that stuff here," my mom would say. She would drag me with her to the sit-ins and protests. We went to one

at Woolworths in Leesburg, which I never forgot. Viviloria also had a mission to integrate the Greyhound bus. There was a black side and a white side, and she believed that we should have access to both. We went to the white side and sat down. I credit her for stirring the activism in my heart. My mother would warn, "Don't get my baby arrested with your foolishness."

I loved her with my whole heart. By the time she became a full adult with children of her own, I found myself traveling to Jacksonville, Florida regularly to help babysit her children.

There was an 11-year difference between my sister Lutricia and me. She was tiny, but she always got her way. Everyone treated her like a princess and she deserved it. She was sweet and kind. She would take me on her dates with her to Dairy Queen, and she never minded that I was a tag-along.

And then there was Basco Thompson, III, my brother, the athlete who was bad to the bone. Without hesitation, I used to advise my mom that wherever she had gotten him from, he deserved to be sent back. His chocolate hue was beautiful but made him a victim to the harsh cruelties of both our community and our white counterparts. Maybe the hatred of the world was at times too much to bear. Either way, he found himself amidst mischief and I wanted nothing to do with any of it.

Do This In Remembrance of You

You must honor you.

You must love you.

You must give to you.

You must comfort you.

You must praise you.

You must teach you.

You must never lose sight of you.

MIND

Pure Thoughts and Good Intentions

"Simply put, problems that need to be solved are illusions of the mind."

-**Beryl McClary**-

Honor the power of your mind, for it has the ability to create heaven on earth or hell within. You must resolve to give the world the best of you as opposed to what's left of you. Plant seeds of prosperity through your thoughts. Your best begins with your mind.

CHAPTER 1
SELF-PERCEPTION

If you stare in the mirror long enough, you are bound to find something to love.

-Beryl McClary-

The way you see yourself matters far greater than the way that others see you.

Strong. Risk-taker. Educator. Protector. Defender. Leader. Committed. Loyal. Confident. Attractive. Faithful.

These are words that you likely identify with, but do you truly believe them to be true? You may have never considered it before, but if you don't have the right perception of yourself, your possibilities in life can and will be limited. You won't be able to do the things you desire to do, and you run the risk of never walking in the abundance of your calling. The key is knowing that your opinion trumps all others. If you're affected by what people think of you, then your perception of yourself will be determined by their opinions rather than honest self-reflection.

When I was in fourth grade, prior to integration, I decided that I wanted to have a part in a school play that was being assembled. I imagined myself in the role and gave little thought to the prospect of not being cast. I was devastated when the teacher told me that I would not be a good fit. Her reasoning was due in part to my stuttering. I was shattered and had not realized that I was being judged based upon limitations of my speech. At the time, schools were not integrated, but I also imagined that had something to do with the devastating outcome. From that day forward, I resolved to engage in activities that would alleviate my stuttering and the option for anyone to deny me any opportunity as a result of it. By the time the schools integrated, I taught myself to speak in public and entered several speech competitions. My first speech was entitled "It's Time for Change." Even though I had been told previously that I could not speak well, I won first place. My father, who also stuttered, was a man of few words, and as I got older, I understood why. I also learned that the teacher had made an inaccurate diagnosis about my speech. The truth was that I didn't stutter, I simply spoke fast.

I was also an avid reader as a little girl. Mom would bring me books and biographies from various black authors and important people. The more I read, the more inspired I became. Many titles I read over and over, as they sparked my interest. The formal address of the celebration of Black History Month had not yet been recognized, but my mother recognized that education and the reality that we had the power to dream of for ourselves went hand in hand. The biographies introduced me to the possibilities of life and encouraged me to reach for more.

The way that you see yourself is not limited to what you can achieve. We must also consider that our physical appearance falls victim to the scrutiny and opinions of others. In high school I never thought I was pretty, and I must have adopted this sentiment as my own in college as well. As opposed to being obsessed with the exterior, I spent my time fixated on thoughts of what I could become. I studied the actions of multimillionaires and entrepreneurs and arrived at the conclusion that whatever it was that they had, I too was born with it. There were times that proved that I might have to work at it more, but I had everything I needed within and it wasn't dependent on anyone's approval or perceptions of me. Not categorizing beauty based upon what others thought of me provided me with a confident assurance. By the time I was enrolled in college, I knew in my heart that who and what I was would be enough for what I was called to do, and being pretty was not one of them. It wasn't until a stroll down memory lane conversation with my nephew caught my attention surrounding the whole beauty in the eye of the beholder theory. He said, "I remember you. You were so pretty." And I was, but I never knew it until I was older. In retrospect, I hated having to be like everybody else in order to succeed, and much of my categorization of beauty aligned with success obtained from work completed. I took great pride in knowing that no one could deny me an opportunity based upon my work ethic. I had the power to control my narrative and my story and in many ways, this rebellion of sorts was a good old fashioned "I told you so" to the teacher who had not cast me in the play back in elementary school. The greatest lesson gleaned was that I had the power to shape my beliefs about myself. That same power is reserved for you. You can either allow someone to make you feel inferior based upon their limited perceptions, or you can take matters into your own hands to establish your own patterns of thought. I recommend the latter.

Disappointment vs. Discovery

It is certain that real life twists and turns can at times feel like a series of disappointments. These moments can play a role in how we perceive ourselves. Disappointment can affect how you perceive your life and your disposition in it. You can feel like things are going wrong, or that you're hopeless or trapped. The simple truth is that you have to assume responsibility for changing your perception. Take control of the things that you can control. You must also be willing to jump over the obstacles placed before you.

Find ways to fill your mind with positive thoughts and resolve that your voice inside must be louder than the countless voices of others outside. The motivational speakers that I believe in say that it's very important to fill yourself with positive thoughts. Sometimes it's music, sometimes it's inspirational quotes from Oprah Winfrey those who lead the charge for higher consciousness and the abundance that life has to offer. You must concern yourself with things that will redirect your thoughts in a positive manner. No one is going to care about your future but you. You may encounter those who offer their help, but ultimately nobody is assigned to your success. There is joy in knowing that you are not alone, even when life appears to isolate you. The good Lord is always there.

I have also resolved that asking the question why yields very little productivity. You can benefit from instead asking questions like... *What should I get out of this? What needs to change?* Not why. Questions like...*How can I make this better, how can I redirect, how can I succeed? How do we move to the next step? How do we take it bit by bit?* This pattern of thought harnesses your energy toward prosperity as opposed to scarcity and doubt. Learn to calm yourself and find moments of strength.

Confidence and the ability to perceive yourself in a positive light must be prefaced in knowing that there is always an answer in your head waiting for you to access it. Calm yourself and trust God. Rest assured that you will have an aha moment. Someone said to get a better answer in life you have to ask better questions.

You can also take into consideration that as you get older, some things become less important. You don't feel the need to prove yourself as much. In your thirties you envision conquering the world. You see others and resolve that *Maybe I can do this too.* As you get older, you realize this is what it is, baby! You focus more on becoming content with who and what you are. The evolution of age and wisdom and grace is not easy but so worth it.

Your Circle of Influence

Chances are if you are reading these words, then you already recognize that your circle of friends, acquaintances and cohorts matters. If you are around negative people, people whose existence is dependent on the approval of others or a perceived status, you inevitably move away from authenticity. Growth and evolution of your self-perception means getting to a point where you need to step back and accept every part of you. That quirk of humor that makes you different also makes you you. There are people that like that about you, don't lose it. I'm not saying that you don't need refining, but you should accept your version of you. I can recall being around the age of twenty-seven and putting myself in a box because I didn't think I was enough. It wasn't until I was older that I realized I am enough. And as much as we'd like to believe that we are our own greatest influences, we are all influenced by those whom we spend time engaging with.

Today, I don't make myself small to make anyone feel better. I'm not afraid to admit that I had to work at that attitude. I encourage you to up your game in this realm of possibility. I also encourage you not to apologize for who you are. I refuse to do so. I'm secure in my tight dresses just like I'm secure in my business suit. I began to recognize the great power in self-acceptance prior to requesting it from others. There will always be criticisms and you should remain open to constructive criticism, but never allow others to define you. Even if others are throwing shade, like who you are. If you don't like who you are, then it is up to you to change. Seek out graciousness; become kind and patient with yourself and others. Embrace Christian values, and you can become empowered to feel good about the lady staring back at you in the mirror. When I go to McDonald's, I make a point of complimenting whoever is at the window. That attitude comes with age. The good thing about getting older is that there is no competition, and that's the best news ever. Imagine showing up to a marathon prepared to race and the officials handing you a medal and telling you that you've already won without ever having placed a foot on the track. Operating as if you have no competition is freeing on another level.

Words Have Power

Another factor that must be considered in how we perceive ourselves is the words that we speak. When we harness the power of our ability to change our thoughts, we tap into divine energy to shape our words. My life changed when I began to practice speaking words of prosperity. My continued studies led me to observe patterns of successful people who had different ways of thinking. As I listened to more stories, one common denominator was recognizing that words have power. I started listening to how they framed things. Their language was rich and different from what I had been using. If something didn't turn out the way they expected, they didn't see it that way. They'd say, "I didn't get the outcome I was in search of, so we will make changes to get another outcome." Your viewpoint differs according to how you frame it. Recognizing that the strategy of powerful words made my self-confidence increase. In this space, I realized that I too had what it took to attain success. You must know that all of the universe wants you to succeed. Equipped with this information, I changed my expectancy from considering what could go wrong today to imagining what doors of opportunity will open up for me today.

A Moment of Reflection

Who Do You Want the World to See You As?

CHAPTER 2
MENTAL HEALTH

Your mental health is the sunshine within. Let no one dim your light.

-**Beryl McClary**-

Your mental health and your emotional well-being go hand in hand. Mental health can affect how you thrive in life. Unhealthy thoughts have the power to immobilize you. My mother would always say, "Watch your thoughts; your thoughts will become words. Watch your words; your words will turn into actions."

After my husband Thomas and I got married, we had an immediate family. Our first daughter was Ashley, who was my wedding present. Although I had not given birth to her, my position to love and care for her began immediately. Very shortly after our nuptials, we discovered that I was pregnant with my firstborn, and the babies kept coming. I had five children in six and a half years and our oldest was my bonus daughter. The first time I gave birth, I was 36 and delivered our last babies (a set of twins) at 42.

As a new mother, I would often get overwhelmed with all the diapers and chores that I was now accountable for overseeing. To propel myself forward, I recognized that I would have to change my patterns of thinking or lose my mind. Instead of viewing the things that I needed to get done as chores, I discovered new ways to make them fun. I turned my to-do list into a game. Everything from doing laundry to exercising became a game. I got so into it that I would inspire the kids to join me. Sometimes, they would have to guess the number of sit-ups Mommy could do or how many pieces of clothing Mommy could fold. Recognizing early on that my mental health and stability was all a matter of perspective opened my eyes to new outcomes that would not have otherwise been possible.

Motives vs. Motivations

Two major considerations for your mental health are motives and motivations. You must take time to engage in an ongoing process of self-examination to determine your needs and desires. An awareness of these factors can help you to better understand the decisions that you are likely to make and the rationale for them. You must know what drives you better than anyone else. It is from this space that you walk into a new level of existing. If you do not accept the opportunities to evaluate yourself effectively, you also run the risk of being unable to accept the constructive criticism of others.

It is equally important to keep in mind that assuming full responsibility for the series of events that happen in your life as a result of decisions that you have made gives you unprecedented power. With maturity, you can greatly benefit from avoiding the blame game and indulging in pity parties, which are a waste of your most valuable time. Allow yourself the freedom to make mistakes. After all, you are human. The growth that you desire comes from making corrections along your life's journey. Balance in all things is key.

Let It Go. Live In the Now.

If I had a dollar for all the times when I was younger that I allowed something from the past to get under my skin, the contents of this book might read a little differently. The truth is that with maturity, I learned one of the most valuable lessons that there is to learn. We have no power over our past, nor should we allow it to have any power over us. Allow that to sink in for a moment. The things that happened to you in your childhood and the days that you survived should not take precedence over what your future has given you the potential to accomplish. Holding on to the past threatens your mental health and overall sustainability. These factors can be even more demeaning if you don't have a spiritual foundation from which to experience life.

My spiritual walk was ordained from a very early age, and I am grateful to have known God all my life. I have walked with him and talked with him and believed in him to provide all my life's needs. And up until recently, I had never questioned God's will or presence in my life. One of the most trying tests of faith for not only me but my entire family came in the form of something that we love and cherish with our whole hearts...music.

My dear husband Thomas along with our entire family found

ourselves in the center of a tumultuous court battle for the right to use The Commodores name. My husband Thomas, founder of the group, never dreamed of having to fight to use an entity that he created. The battle went on for years on end and affected everything from our family's finances to future plans. We spent our days in and out of court, on the phones with attorneys and in prayer. To this day, I still don't know how we remembered to breathe. It was a gruesome experience to watch someone you love so dearly be so viciously attacked by those who had once shown brotherly love. The most profound factor was that we wanted nothing from anyone. Our only ask in all of this has been that those involved with the case not bring harm to Thomas' ability to work.

There were so many times I asked God why? There were so many moments when I declared victory that never surfaced. In the end, I had to remember that God sits on the throne and his decisions are just, even if we don't agree or understand. It took experiencing unprecedented heartbreak to serve as a reminder that God will never leave nor forsake us. Had we not had a faith walk, I'm sure things would have turned out much differently.

The unequivocal truth is that life is difficult if you don't believe in anything. To look within ourselves for all of the answers can at times feel like too great of a responsibility. Reading and meditating on the word of God has allowed me to come to peace with things that were meant to destroy me. Attacks on my family don't have any power or authority over us when we casted our troubles to the Lord. Today, we reap the benefits of letting go and living in the now.

Resolving to live in the now empowers you to frame your situation and the outcomes respectively. If you learn to corral your emotions before making a decision, things will work out victoriously. I stand on that.

There is another lesson to be learned in letting go and living in the now. Solutions are all that matter. You can spend hours on end mulling over spilled milk, or you can pick yourself up, dust yourself off and muster up enough determination and grit to problem-solve your way through to prosperity. Consider how you view the situation at hand and what redirection might be needed to be applied. Always remember that most of the things that you see in front of you are temporary and subject to change. As they say...Trouble don't last always. Knowing and believing this single sentiment is the key to remaining open to life's possibilities and thriving in a healthy mental state.

A Moment of Reflection

What steps can you take to remain mentally healthy?

_____
_____
_____
_____
_____
_____
_____
_____
_____
_____
_____
_____
_____
_____
_____
_____
_____

CHAPTER 3
PERCEPTION OF THE WORLD

Life is filled with magical moments, waiting for us to become believers.

-**Beryl McClary**-

Your perception of the world is the way you have experienced it and what you have been exposed to that determines the lens with which you see. It gives you an insight into what really makes a difference as well as the things that should not be allowed to take up space in your heart and mind.

My first lessons about perception (as an adult) that defined the trajectory of my life can be traced to the summer of 1980. After working relentlessly in college to reach what I felt to be my highest potential and being accepted into law school, I was forced to leave. My daddy was dying of cancer. The news was a shock to me, as I had no idea that he was even sick. During my time caring for him, he still managed to hide just how much he was going through. Each day, he would wait until Mom went to work in the afternoons to express the tremendous amount of pain he was experiencing and how much he wanted to die. Leukemia was slowly stealing his life and his joy. In addition to caring for my daddy, it felt as though I spent the entire summer with a mop in my hand attempting to keep the floor clean, as he couldn't hold his urine. My heart ached for him, and I felt helpless, as all I could do was attempt to make him comfortable.

After the summer ended, my mother encouraged me to return to school. In my mind, everything had changed. From my perception of myself, to my family and the world, things were just different. My work ethic had always been driven by a will to perform in excellence, but my grades were better. I was less focused on the competition next to me; I only wanted to be the best that I could be. In previous years, I felt the need to compete with my classmates for academic excellence, but after witnessing my father drift away, while powerless, my perception and understanding of the things that previously stressed me were now minuscule. There were so many things in life that no longer made a difference to me. My understanding of what I was working for was now more clear, and I understood that tomorrow was never promised. The sentiments of empathy and compassion had new meaning in my heart.

When my daddy passed away, a piece of my heart went with him that I knew I would never get back. I found my own ways of coping, but I didn't carry the loss with me; I carried the memories. I accepted that he was gone but also the challenge that I know he would have issued me to keep moving. My perception of his passing was that of transition. Spending the time with him amidst the summer that I returned home to care for him helped me to know that his earthly transition was also his heavenly ascension. The pain that once held him captive was gone. My heart never stopped hearing all the things he would've said had he been living. And in that space, I had the will power and blessing of remaining focused on the good times.

Storms Run Out of Rain

There are some storms of life that are destructive, and others that serve to clear your path. After surviving the tragic passing of my daddy, another unforeseen storm was on the horizon.

A routine visit to the doctor resulted in a call back to advise that I had Graves' disease. Having never heard of the disease, or its symptoms or effects, I was clueless as to how to move forward. I was advised to come in immediately for radioactive treatment. If you listen to your body, it will always reveal what you need to know. I knew that something was wrong as my hair had begun to fall out by the handfuls. My memory was also affected and I had bouts of extreme fatigue. Anyone that dared see their way through law school would understand that, aside from the hair loss, these symptoms were normal. I also took radioactive enzymes. There were so many things that I didn't notice. My neck was thickening and it was also affecting my eyes. Quite possibly other people around me noticed that my eyes looked different, but none of them mentioned it to me. Throughout the process, I learned that the way I managed stress needed to be addressed. Implementing exercise into my daily regimen also served me well. What I did not know at the time was how or when it could resurface.

The professors at the school allowed me to take some exams later (in law school) and I just pushed through it as best as I could. The disease had been taking a toll on me and I was completely unaware.

Law school was a horrific experience at the time and I just wanted to finish. My grades were compromised because I was not healthy. It was very trying because I didn't know what was bringing my grades down. It wasn't me being slack or lazy. There was indeed a legitimate excuse for not being on my game. Prayer became my saving grace. I had experienced yet another shift in my perception and God was my tour guide for every part of life. My final year of law school turned out to be extremely good, but only because God led me through it. Oddly enough, many of my cohorts didn't go to church, but by the end of the semester, we were all there. The storm of Graves' disease had come to clear my path, and once again, God was at the forefront of everything.

Exposure and Experience Are Among the Greatest Teachers

Lack of exposure is one of the major factors that can affect your perception of the world.

There's no way to build a full life if you never get out and experience what else the world has to offer. You can sit and watch the news and have friends with narrow opinions, but that's a very limited life. You need to get out there and get involved with other people outside of your circle, and those who don't necessarily agree with your perspective. I can honestly say that I understand multiple sides of a perspective because I've allowed myself to be exposed to the world and I remain open to what's new. Sometimes you just need to listen and be around others. We are a conglomerate and that is something that should be appreciated. The more you are exposed to, the more your knowledge and perspective grows. Experiential living should be at the top of your bucket list.

It must also be stated that perception of the world changes over time. My compassion has increased and the way I see change is more practical, but that only came with real life experience. I'm able to identify with more people and be of service to more people because I have chosen not to limit my options in terms of who I associate with and the places that I go. My awareness is heightened. It should also be mentioned that you can become more skeptical because of what you know. As you get older, you don't take things at face value. What you have been taught can affect your behavior. I just believe that we are the world and that we cannot separate ourselves from the experiences and people that the world has to offer. I often tell young people that if you feel a void in your life, it's not outside but inside, that you must discover the deficit and then find the experience that you need to fill it. Experience and exposure are plentiful teachers.

A Full Spirit

How do you fill your spirit? Believe it or not, it doesn't take much. You are three parts: the flesh, the feelings, and the spirit. These three entities are the reason that when you close your eyes you can feel warmth. I choose to fill my spirit with God and I choose to believe in God. Life is too hard not to believe in something greater. Imagine for a minute you believe in nothing. How do you feel? I'd venture to say empty. That void is what so many people in the world are experiencing. Do you ever see the sun get confused about who or what to follow? It rises in the east and sets in the west and it dares to shine. You must adopt this same spirit of existence and being for your life. Your perception will always be a reflection of the fullness of your soul. Drop every fear and pick up faith—it is yours for the taking!

A Moment of Reflection

What action can you take to alleviate your most limiting belief in life?

CHAPTER 4
STAYING SHARP

To experience life, the mind should be two things, free and on fire.

-Beryl McClary-

Staying sharp means remaining relevant and knowledgeable. Figuring out what's going on around you and what's going on in the world must not be optional. Seeking new ideas about the here and now and remaining abreast of current events are all intricate acts to remain sharp at all times. There are no age limits that denote that you are no longer able to be on the cutting edge of information, ideas or technology, therefore, no barriers should be placed upon your ability to do so. What was effective yesterday might not be effective today, and that's perfectly fine. Keeping yourself current can make the transitions and changes less dramatic along the way. Being too busy for everyday life threatens your ability to remain up to date. In order to stay sharp, you have to make a conscious effort to grow and evolve.

Knowledge is Power

Making deliberate time to educate yourself is critical. Commit time to sitting down and reading current magazines and books. Engage with new ways of thinking. It takes time to learn new things and it takes even more time to apply what you have learned. Give yourself permission to be new and to explore the unknown. You also have to watch out for procrastination, as it creeps in over the years and turns your will into woulda coulda shouldas.

At the end of the day, remaining sharp comes down to discipline. No matter how your life progresses, you still have the same 24 hours a day that you had when you were much younger. One of the statements that I often make to my children is, everything is a matter of time spent. Ask yourself, what you are doing with the hours of time that you have been gifted? Even now, I still begin my day with intentional acts. I still set individual goals every day. At the end of the day, I look back to access what time I wasted. It's all about intention and focus.

Also, do keep in mind that your needs change over time depending on where you are occupationally. I can work more toward my goals because I am a business person, which is different from someone who is retired. Many people read the New York Times and the Wall Street Journal for breakfast. In my line of work as an attorney, it is definite that I know what is happening globally and nationally. Setting long-term goals is also a way to challenge the levels of complacency that can settle in when not monitored. I even go as far as establishing goals for the next ten years. I don't, nor have I ever just wanted to exist. I desire to impact the world in a way that contributes to the discovery and execution of greatness in others.

A Word About Intuition

Although I am not stating that spirituality plays a role in staying sharp, the spirit of wisdom, which is a derivative of your spirituality, does. I don't think your spirituality and your actuality can be separated. The spirit of wisdom is what ignites your intuition, a divine enlightening that you can't afford to live without.

The Art of Conscious Conversation

It's important to spend time around people who are sharp and to engage in conversations that trigger you to think. Surrounding yourself with people who are smarter than you is also key. The goal is to remain in a constant state of learning, not to be the smartest person in the room. It is my desire to be around thinkers. You will become like those you keep around you.

Just Do It

Prior to taking the leap of faith into entrepreneurship and even during the process of writing this book, there were periods that I had to learn about the power of marketing and making connections. At each juncture, I realized that my knowledge of branding needed to be updated. As the wife of a world-renowned musician who took an active role in the oversight and often management of business affairs, I did recognize that I had been blessed to have more on-the-job training than I had given myself credit for; however, I also recognized that best practices and strategies in business are ever changing. For me, staying sharp meant committing to exploring the possibilities and learning new and innovative practices. As a self-proclaimed voracious reader, I read every magazine for entrepreneurs that I could get my hands on. Learning how other entrepreneurs navigated business taught me a great deal. My ever inquisitive mind pondered questions like, what do they do to achieve their dreams? How do they navigate the waters when the market or their industry is going down? The research on my part was ongoing. As I see it, the two things that you can't have too much of are money and information.

Not all of the information that I came across propelled me further. Some was just fluff, but either way, I took the time to access the information. Another strategy that I implemented was reading about those who were on their journeys toward success. I didn't read about those who had already made it. My curiosity was rooted in those who dared to survive while in pursuit of their dreams, which is by far one of the most difficult and rewarding places to be in life.

What I had recognized over the years was that law school taught me how to decode the law. What it had not taught me was how to decode best business practices. To accommodate this deficit, I also enrolled in online courses. There were so many lawyers in the world, but I intended on making my voice and my work heard and seen. Staying abreast of the ever changing world in front of you is the absolute best way to remain in active pursuit of life. Staying sharp is about not allowing life to happen to you but being aware and present such that you chase your destiny and use all of your days by filling them with purpose.

A Moment of Reflection

Why is it necessary to exercise your mind on a continual basis?

CHAPTER 5
TECH

If you don't plan to learn, then you don't plan to live.

-Beryl McClary-

In this day and age, there can be no excuses for not getting things done. Moreover, with increased technology at our fingertips, productivity is enhanced. At this point, I would venture to say that there is not a person in the world who has not been impacted by technological advances. From connecting with friends and loved ones from far away to creating music and content in every format and increasing our knowledge, technology has changed and shaped our lives in ways unimaginable.

Balance in All Things

And although we have the element of convenience at our fingertips, I do believe that we must discover balance. It is possible that we cheat ourselves of the opportunities to think on our own when our usage is out of balance. I've seen cashiers who aren't able to add or subtract without the computer. It can also make you lazy so that you don't go out and do your own in-depth research to discover information that you need or desire to learn. We must not forget that information you get online can be skewed. You have to guard yourself against other people's thoughts and opinions that are thrust on you. And as you become seasoned, you must maintain balance with anything that discourages critical thinking. I want for us to never become complacent in relying on information without thinking about the source. There are questions that you should ask and fuel your inquisitive side.

Reach Out and Touch Somebody's Hand

No matter how much you immerse yourself in the use of technology, never lose sight of the power of human interaction. Although some won't admit to this, the truth is that feelings can be disabled by technology, therefore limiting your actual experiences. Admittedly, there was a time that I became preoccupied by the computer. I felt like I couldn't get up; I had to keep reading and engaging. There were months where I was so immersed and saturated that my legs would ache from sitting too long and my eyes would get blurry. I found myself at the computer for 10 hours of the day, completely preoccupied trying to sift through the information. I was very focused. At the time, that computer owned me. Things got to the point where I didn't want to engage as frequently with others because I was preoccupied all the time. I was having conference calls two to three times a week and they consumed me. Many of the calls were at night, which also cut into time spent with family.

There came a point in which I finally realized that I wasn't interacting with my family as often or getting any exercise, and I knew that something would have to change. I made the decision to redirect my entertainment and my allocation of time. I also took the initiative to examine the root cause of my engagement with technology. My internal investigation revealed that at the time, I felt as though I was behind with some of the personal goals that I had set in motion both personally and professionally. To the outside world, things likely appeared that I was thriving, and I was, but my personal plans were slightly off schedule and I was too hard on myself. I'm very cautious about that now and taking time to recognize areas to seek balance empowered me in ways that I didn't know to be possible.

Today, I allocate a schedule for my use of technology. Every two hours I stand up and do something else. I no longer engage for excessively long intervals with the computer.

You must be watchful of your time, as it is a precious resource that you will not get back once used. Most importantly, never forget that technology should never be used to replace human connection.

Commit to Communication

As much as technology connects us, it can also do the exact opposite by limiting our exchanges to phones and computers, further isolating us from those we should be spending quality time with. To combat this scenario, you must learn when to turn technology off. Establishing non-negotiable areas has served as a way for me to ensure that I am not missing out on valuable moments to commit to communication. One of those places for me is the bedroom. On many occasions, I have recommended to my children that they power their devices off so that they are not scrolling in the middle of the night. We have all been guilty of checking our phones at times that seem unjustifiable; the question becomes how then, do we seek balance? Although it may sound drastic to some, I have also leveraged the option to leave my phone while in the office or the car. You have to find a way to separate yourself from your technology in locations that you wish to engage or be at peace with your thoughts.

Another hidden factor that is not discussed is how the use of technology has the potential to make us immobile. When we work all of the time and don't make space for the creation of genuine interaction, our energy, actions, intentions and time is consumed with the use of technology. Simply stated, you have to put a limit on it.

Commit to Learning

Even with all that has been mentioned about technology, its uses and the factors that can prove to be detrimental from a lack of balance, I would be remiss if I did not speak about the value in using technology to propel you forward. As a lifelong learner, there has never been such a time to access information so freely. The internet has empowered us to acquire knowledge about anything we so choose and in many instances at no additional cost, other than the fees paid for subscription to wifi or cellular services. Technology is all around us and it behooves us to remain abreast of the various ways to leverage it to our advantage.

Technology can also be used for inspiration. At your fingertips, you have access to videos and content intended to ignite the fire inside of you to do and be more. From writers, digital content creators, spiritual leaders, financial advisors and entrepreneurs, there is no shortage of information or content to make you feel good.

At the end of the day, you must never stop learning, growing and seeking new ways to use the new developments that are created. As I see it, remaining current is not an option, it is the only option.

A Moment of Reflection

If you could learn about a new advancement in technology without limits, what would you choose to learn about?

25

BODY

A Work of Art

Some people pray for miracles. I pray for a long life and good health. I know that God will supply everything else.

-**Beryl McClary**-

Your body is your vessel. It is your responsibility to ensure that it is protected, nourished, and replenished at all times. No one will do this for you, nor should it be your expectation. You must never forget that you will only be given one vessel, so treat it well.

CHAPTER 6
EXERCISE

Exercise is a blessing not a chore.

-**Beryl McClary**-

When things in my life become overbearing, I take a run until my viewpoint changes. I have determined that engaging my body while allowing it to support the thoughts that flow through my mind is an act of healing.

There was a time that I had gotten up to about 185 pounds. I can't say that I felt the absolute best about myself but I was also a doting wife and raising several small children simultaneously. I can recall attending social events and some of my husband's friends and acquaintances had remarried. Many had younger and what I believed to be stunning girlfriends. They had beautiful clothes, size 6 frames, perky boobs and flat stomachs. Watching them with their sultry poses, I somehow couldn't help but to compare myself. In truth, I believe that any regular mother like me would have made the comparison. My hands were busy and filled with babies. It was all that I could do to find two matching shoes. It hurts to admit, but I didn't feel good about myself. When I got married at age 35, I was wearing a size 7, but life happened. And although it was the life that I loved, I had managed to lose myself in it. I was carrying babies at ages 36, 37, 38, 39, 41, 42. I can remember just wanting to wear a belt. My waistline as I had known it was no longer one that I recognized.

Around that same era on another occasion, I had gone to the dentist's office for a routine cleaning. After my appointment ended, I was passing by a long mirror and I saw myself. I was wearing this long khaki skirt and the mirror was brutally honest with me. I was wearing a longer skirt to hide the fat. The closer I looked and the half hearted spin, revealed my rear. I had never had much of a rear but I could not believe how much I had acquired. I had to stop to wonder who was walking behind me. The social engagements and the routine occurrences of life, such as visits to the doctor were both

bold reminders of the weight that I had gained. I only expressed my concerns to my good friend. She would say, "Beryl, embrace whatever weight you are." I knew she was right but I didn't feel pretty. The straw that broke the camel's back was when my husband Thomas began to play with the fat on my stomach. I was livid. I had tried to embrace the fat but I never believed it to be mine to keep.

Once and for all, I made up my mind to fight fire with fire. As God would have it, my law office was situated one block away from a park downtown. During court proceedings, I used frustration to fuel my fight with fat. Every time opposing counsel responded in an ugly way, I would grab my tennis shoes and take a walk. As I saw it, the factors of my life that kept me busy and engaged were not going to change. I had a choice to either get bigger or to turn things around for myself. The pressures of the cases caused me to get out and take a walk. The more motions and pleas made, the more I redirected the energy towards something that would make me more healthy as opposed to sick.

Over time, the slow paced walks introduced me to swifter paces and before I knew it, I was running. After about a year of running to relieve me from my mental and physical bondage, I had lost all of the weight. I was working so hard. Instead of just bringing my tennis shoes to work, I was bringing all of my running gear. I would leave my suit in the car until it would be time for me to go to the trial. That year, I won a major case and discovered personal and professional victory. I felt better.

Feeling better about myself, empowered me to have more to give to others. The act of running gave me clarity and allowed me time to pray. It was amidst those prayers that I received answers to difficult questions and guidance to make difficult decisions. Running allowed me to hear directly from God. On some occasions, I listened to podcasts, motivational sermons, and scriptures and on other occasions, I got quiet enough to hear my own voice. The truth is that I don't hear from God at my desk or when I am busy with my day, but somewhere around the 4th or 5th mile, I can hear God speak so clearly. Running allows me to remain centered on him and calms my heart.

Today, I try to cover so many miles a week and I don't place any limits on what I have the potential to achieve physically. I run at least four or five times a week and I make no apologies for taking that time to better myself. Over the years, I have also incorporated weight lifting, mostly to keep the bat wings down. There are days that I will also put on a waist cincher or a binder. When you sit at a computer, you tend to let your stomach muscles go. The first time I tried one on, it did pinch and I couldn't breathe, but I must say that it works.

Running has now become one of the most enjoyable times of my day. Even while on vacation, I still run because it is absolutely torturous not to. If I'm indoors, I will probably do floor exercises or lift weights to keep my body in motion and fighting to reach a goal.

Small goals become larger goals and the achievement of them helps you to discover your own strength. My next level in fitness was running races in support of good causes. Tying my personal goals in with the act of being purposeful has made me whole. In life, it is always easier to be giving. My goal of accomplishing my first half-marathon really strengthened me. I hadn't done a half-marathon before and was not certain of if I could achieve such a monstrous feat. I can remember hosting a vision board party. While at the party, I cut out an advertisement for a half marathon and a person who was crossing the finish line. I traveled with that photo. As that year was coming to an end, I still had not accomplished the goal, which was fuel for my ambition. I was determined. The day before one of the last races of the year, I registered. The event coordinators hate when you do that, but this goal was for me. The next day, there I was going up the bridge, and dashing through the city. And even though I was in the race, I hadn't been training like I should have to prepare for a race of that magnitude. Somewhere around the eleventh mile, I could feel my body wanting to give up. The total race was a twelve-mile run. Prior to that, I had not done anything above four to six miles. It was there in that eleventh mile that I could barely lift my legs. I struggled to cross the finish line, but by the grace of God I did. I knew from that moment on that I owed it to myself to ensure my mind and body be prepared for the ambitions of my heart. Overall, the races are a lot of fun and give you the opportunity to meet a lot of people who are inspirational. There are other women there who are in good shape, and those who have amazing times to inspire you to keep improving.

Currently, I try to do at least one or two half marathons per year. The ones by the ocean are my favorite. Through it all, exercise must be a personal experience. I don't believe that anyone could have made me more of a believer in myself and my abilities than I could have done. When it comes to fitness, you have to ask yourself what you desire? After doing so, there are many things to consider. What are the factors of your life that threaten your ability to exercise? If you don't discipline yourself, you won't follow through. If I put it off exercising because I work too late or if I don't make an effort to work out during my lunch hour, things get fuzzy. Small, intentional moves such as keeping a bag in my car with extra exercise clothes helps me to alleviate excuses. Weather can also be a concern or an excuse. I live in Florida, where we have many 100 degree days. It's really hard for me to run if the temperature is over 88 degrees. If I can't run for some reason, then I also have goals set to make sure I get a sufficient amount of steps in. I use an app on my phone that keeps me on track. If for any reason, I do not get sufficient steps completed, I make up for it the next day. Here is the thing, in most instances if you're hiding from the scale, you're hiding from something else in your life. Your exercise and the way that you treat your body is a by-product of your accountability to yourself. We must all resolve to be accountable for our bodies. I have also learned over the years to avoid people who don't care about fitness. You need friends who are more conscious, or at the very least, like-minded. You have to have people in your circle that understand and are supportive versus those encouraging you to eat the chips over the carrots. If you choose a workout partner, let it be someone who will not make excuses for getting to the gym. Accountability in the large and small matters make all the difference. My advice is to be inspired by everything and allow it to encourage you to get up and move your body. The whole world is your playground, go out and play.

Fitness for the Fierce

Even if you can't make it to the gym, all hope is not lost. It is my belief that you can use what you have to accomplish your goals. Here is my week long exercise regime for the days that fitness forgoes four walls. To perform these exercises, all you need is you.

Day I:

- 60 Second Plank
- 20 Jumping Jacks
- 10 Pushups
- 20 Lunges
- 10 Russian Twists

Day II:

- 60 Second Plank
- 20 Speed Skaters
- 10 Pushups
- 20 Lunges
- 10 Russian Twists

Day III:

- 60 Second Plank
- 20 Speed Skaters
- 10 Pushups
- 20 Squats
- 10 Russian Twists
- Bicycle Crunches

Day IV:

- 60 Second Plank
- 20 Butt Kicks
- 10 Pushups
- 20 Squats
- 10 Russian Twists
- 10 Bicycle Crunches

Day VI:

- 60 Second Plank
- 20 Butt Kicks
- 10 Pushups
- 20 Squats
- 10 Russian Twists
- 10 Bicycle Crunches
- 10 Full Sit Ups

CHAPTER 7
NUTRITION

You can only be healthy on the outside if you make it a priority to be healthy on the inside first.

-Beryl McClary-

When it comes to food, I have one goal, to enjoy it. Experience has taught me that I have the power to do what is best for my health while still enjoying the food that I put in it. That choice led me to become a pro in my research to discover meals that tasted good but were also nourishing. As the mother of seven children, I had to be practical. Let's face it, the kids were not going to eat if they didn't believe that the food tasted good. I began taking some time to peruse cookbooks at leisure. Asking the children to look through the books with me to find recipes or foods they would eat proved to be a massive win. It goes without saying that they like to eat. Prior to leveraging the cookbook strategy, I was in search of a refresh of meals to prepare for the family. When you cook as much as I did, you run out of options. By the time we finished our cookbook adventures, I had great thirty-minute meals and a host of recipes that the entire family could enjoy. I used as many fresh products as possible. Olive oil became my best friend. Fresh herbs such as cilantro and oregano were always on hand for added flavor. Although I ate a lot of seafood, my children prefered chicken. We were all in motion so much that they didn't even realize that they were eating healthy. We made so many meals that were not only tasty, but also low fat and low carbs. It is my belief that food is more filling when you make it yourself. When you go out, the satisfaction is almost always temporary. No matter how much we want to eat at home, we must also learn how to eat for nourishment when we are away from home. On the days that I went into the office, I would open a can of soup and eat at my desk. On occasions when I would go out for lunch with my colleagues, I would order the soup at a nearby Thai restaurant. The broth and spring rolls worked well for my diet and fitness goals. Soups are a great way to keep weight down.

Nutrition affects our ability to thrive in life. Practicing healthy nutrition keeps you from being sick and keeps your body strong and your skin glowing. Although many people inquire about my regimens, admittedly, I don't do anything special. I consistently drink lots of water and watch what I eat. The food that we consume has immense power and we must remain vigilant in how what we consume affects us. Be aware of foods that make you tired. Be aware of what medications are you taking and if there are any ways to remedy ailments by altering your diet? So many things can be traced to what we have eaten. I avoid empty calories as much as possible. I avoid diet drinks at all costs. I believe that artificial ingredients are small sources of internal destruction. Even when cooking spaghetti, I would get tomatoes and blend my own sauce. My family appreciated my efforts to prepare meals that they would enjoy, and I appreciated being a mom who could cook. It's not easy to cook consciously but I am proof that it is possible. As a result of my efforts, my children consumed fewer desserts than I did because they were full from their food, a major score for a parent.

Preparing to Eat

Not preparing to eat is detrimental to your nutritional health. There are so many distractions and the world is so busy that far too often, you could find yourself grabbing for the first thing that is available if you are hungry. That something can end up being french fries, chips or foods from fast food restaurants that were not engineered for your health. I can remember forgetting to take items out of the freezer before leaving for work on occasions, which would send me into a frenzy trying to pull something together for everyone to eat. Another factor that can make you forgo even the best plans for a healthy lifestyle is stress. If I am stressed, sweets would calm me down. I can have one but I am far more capable of having three. For me preparation for nutrition also meant being mindful of stress. Negative situations can trigger your eating habits if you allow them to do so. Preparation will help with this. Bring the carrots and almonds with you. Keep snacks that feed your spirit and your body with you. Place food where it is readily available. It is also imperative that you make it a priority to eat several times a day. I always have something to put my hands on. Nutrition is so much harder without options. You need options. The family won't eat as much fast food and junk food if a healthy meal is ready when they walk in the door. There were times that I would go straight from my car into the house, take off my shoes, and start cooking to make sure that I placed health options at the top of our priority list. Preparation is the key to eating well.

Reclaim Your Power

Remain open to trying new things but do not eat foods that don't taste good to you. Find your way around the kitchen and make it your playground. Eating a nutritionally balanced diet does not have to feel as though you are eating cardboard. The key is to find time and space to treat yourself to the healthy options that make you happy. Find ways to motivate yourself, such as reading content that emphasizes healthy lifestyles. As you pass through the magazine aisle in the grocery store, grab something that captures your attention. Doing so allows you to reflect on what you've eaten and gather ideas for new and improved meals. Take time to write down everything you eat so that you can have a clear view of everything. Whatever you do, reclaim your diet and reclaim your power. Your health is your wealth.

Beryl's Recipes for The Next Chapter

My recipes are what saved my life. Allow me to share a few of them with you. Discover your power in your pots!

Disclaimer: I don't believe in measuring, I believe in cooking that feels good. The recipes featured do not have specific amounts. I encourage you to season to taste and most importantly to cook with love.

Slow Cooked Vegetable Soup for Divas Only

Ingredients
- Fresh Zucchini
- Corn
- Green Beans
- Celery
- Onion
- Carrots
- Cabbage
- Green and Red Peppers
- Vegetable Broth
- Paprika
- Dried Herbs
- Pink Himilayan Salt
- Vegetable Stock
- Olive Oil
- Fresh Dill (As a Topping)

Wash and drain all vegetables and set them aside. In a crock pot, pour vegetable stock, dried herbs and paprika and stir. Add a pinch of pink himilayan salt and a half cup of olive oil to the pot. Turn the crock pot onto the low setting. Allow to steam for approximately 15 minutes with the lid on. Combine all vegetables to the steaming pot and cover with the lid. Return to stir, periodically, making sure that all vegetables are covered by the broth. Taste the broth to see if you wish to add more of the dry seasonings or salt. Keep in mind that your soup will taste more salty as it cooks. When vegetables are tender to your liking, garnish with dill. Viola!

CHAPTER 8
FASHION

You are the canvas and fashion is the work of art.

-**Beryl McClary**-

Fashion to me is to be relevant, modern, sophisticated, and intentional. Fashion does not reflect age, yet it has the power to speak of one's grace. For me, fashion is my moment to be unapologetic about who I am and the pieces of me that I deem worthy of celebrating. I have resolved to not conform to the standard of what anyone else may have set for me. In so many ways society has always had a hand in dictating who and what a woman should be and moreover what she should wear. For far too long women have been imprisoned by imposed standards of what certain attire communicates to the world about their internal composition. Leaning more towards a free spirited approach, I have learned to use fashion as resistance to the status quo. I dress for me and nobody else. When I decide to wear something, it is for one reason, it makes me feel good. I have no concern for what anyone might say or think. This approach is so liberating. And although today, I bask in the freedom of fashion, this has not always been the case.

After having children, I had that frumpy mom look. The weight gain didn't make it any better. At the time had someone asked, I'm almost certain that I would have proclaimed that fashion and clothing was a burden to me. While shopping on the few occasions that I purchased items for myself, I would get the first thing I saw and hate it later. I also recognize that I was very self-conscious during that time. I didn't know enough about fashion and style to work it or should I say, to make it work for me. I couldn't go out and wear the most expensive pieces because we had seven children who were in private school and what seemed like every activity that existed. In my opinion, I always looked frazzled. In retrospect, it wasn't just the clothes, I also needed to find me. What we wear has much to do with what's on the inside, whether we choose to openly admit it or not.

My husband who has always had an eye for art, both musically and as expressed through his fashion is a gentle reminder that clothes are wearable art. He has an eye for color and knows how to make a statement. After all of his years in the entertainment industry, I would expect no less. Watching him put colors together has served as a source of encouragement to me. Color has the power to mirror our souls and make us look beautiful.

Embrace Evolution

The moment I got honest with myself and acknowledged my look of old as frumpy, I knew that I had to reprioritize yet again in another area of my life. Much like my physical appearance, health and nutrition, I decided to make myself a priority in the way that I dressed. And while I don't believe that we should allow the world to dictate who we are, we can not deny that we will be judged by how we show up. When the time came to do away with the khakis and long, unflattering skirts, I hired a personal stylist. I knew that the help I needed was beyond what I could craft on my own. The stylist brought many apparel suggestions, and taught me a great deal about cuts that worked for my body type. She encouraged me through discussions about clothing, but there was a notable amount of internal work taking place simultaneously.

A Word About Unmentionables

I have always believed in undergarments. When I worked with the stylist, she brought things that flattered me. Clothes that flatter your body type paired with the proper undergarments can take your appearance to the next level. No matter how old you are, what you wear underneath still matters. I've also discovered that what you put on underneath your clothes, considering that it does not cut off your circulation or compromise your ability to breathe can also affect the way that you feel outwardly. Fashion and feeling good are an inside job first.

Style Should Not Be Lost, Only Discovered

Getting older does not mean losing your sense of style. This sentence is me screaming from the rooftops to implore that as women, no matter the age, we own the right to look and feel our absolute best. If you're getting older or you've gained weight, determine what you want to have happen in your life. There are fashion options for every size and a plethora of ways for every single one of us to dress in a way that highlights the areas we are most proud of and disguise the ones that we would rather be left alone about. My mother used to always say that "the first thing a woman should do when she wakes up is put on makeup." She meant what you're wearing reflects how you feel about yourself. Prior to working with a stylist, I had no idea that I could have had my jacket tailored to create a more profound waistline. I had no idea that color was power. If I had been more passionate about my presentation, I would have worn more vibrant clothes. We do not have to hide under black. Even before we are all that we are to others, we deserve to first be happy, healthy and whole for ourselves.

A Little Glamour Goes A Long Ways

Fashion and a sense of style can also be discovered in the details. Adding that hint of sparkle or scarf that you thought twice about just might be the thing that makes you feel good. Add a little makeup on the face if that is what will make your mood better. People will say you look good, but more importantly, you will feel good. And although many will fail to admit it, there is nothing like getting complimented. Try a pair of colored shoes. I still wear three or four inches, if that's what I feel like doing.

I feel qualified to encourage women in this space because when I look at old photos, there are times that I can't believe it was me. What I see in those photos today is a woman who was exhausted. I just laugh. That being said, I can't believe I allowed myself to get to that level. I remember my niece saying, "Auntie, don't you want to put on some makeup or something?" I'm glad she brought that to my attention. Sometimes we don't know what to do to get out of that fog. That's when you get someone to help you so they can make what you walk in sparkle. Every woman deserves a hint of sparkle.

Defining You

Fashion Rule #1: Don't let anyone define you. I don't know if you can do that in your 30s but the more seasoned you become, the less value you find in the opinions of others. It is imperative that you like who you are even with the faults because it shows up in what you wear. And even on those occasions when people are bold enough to point out your faults, try not to take it personally. Much of what others have to say is more a reflection of them than it is of you.

Watching people own who they are and it manifest in what they wear is empowering. One young lady in my family stated that she liked being *thick*, a term we use in the south to describe a person with a little meat on their bones. She was an athlete and she had no problem wearing her bikini in a size twenty. I was wearing a T-shirt because I was embarrassed. Part of style it is accepting who you are in the moment and maximizing that. As we grow older, we morph and evolve. We must learn to embrace the beauty of evolution to discover the best versions of ourselves.

Be Open to Learn

Hiring a stylist was a wonderful turning point in my life. Although you have to have a budget, it is an investment in self. She was able to grasp the fact that I didn't want to blend in. It's okay to make fashion statements that are outside of the box if they flatter you. Standing out of the sandbox doesn't mean looking like a clown. It is my belief that every woman deserves to create a style of their own that is both sophisticated and sassy. Modern doesn't necessarily mean trendy. It's not my desire to wear what my 19-year-old twins wear. It's not my desire to wear midriffs. It is also not my desire to show up in the world as if I don't care about my appearance, because it does matter to me.

If you don't know how to redesign your current wardrobe or to select new pieces, ask for someone's help. Stylists who understand sophistication know how to bring out your best without you looking artificial. Today, my look is modern, a bit sassy, and yes, even a bit sexy. If a top is too low, I will get it altered. If an ensemble needs a pop of color, I don't hesitate to add it, but these were all concepts that I had to learn.

Find Inspiration

Inspiration is everywhere. We live in a time where there is photographic evidence of everything, especially fashion. From magazines and media in print to social media, fashion is at our fingertips. I find inspiration in Michelle Obama. Her fashion statements spoke to me as a black woman who was attuned to her femininity and power. I am so proud of her display. Not only does she look good, but she is always appropriate. She is an example of how one can be a style icon but also maintain her individuality. Seeing her during her time as the First Lady as well as amidst her book tours and series of interviews was a gentle reminder that we must all dress up and show up for ourselves.

And while I can't confirm that there is data to prove that fashion affects your ability to thrive, I would be willing to put money on it.

Own the Room

Fashion Rule #2: What you wear affects how others perceive you. We would all like to appease ourselves by proclaiming that outer appearance does not matter, but this simply is not true. We are judged by what we have on and our overall presentation. Likewise, we place judgment based on these same factors. It does not make someone a bad person to form an opinion based upon what they see. At first encounter, the appearance is usually the only information that we have from which to make a judgment. Taking greater pride in what I had on, almost instantly gave me greater credibility. My resume speaks for itself, but I also recognize that my appearance also serves as a viable spokesperson. When you are proud about what you are wearing, you own the room because you are confident. In this space, you are not arrogant, just sure of yourself, and this must be the ultimate goal. What you wear communicates to the world who you are.

CHAPTER 9
RECHARGING

If electronics need to be recharged, so do souls.

-**Beryl McClary**-

Recharging means prioritizing time to refocus and energize your mind, body and soul. During times of recharging, I work diligently to bring myself back to remembrance of what's most important and the goals that I wish to achieve. Like most of us, there are times when life becomes overwhelming and amidst those times, I become scattered in the execution of efforts that some might refer to as multitasking. It is during these times that I feel overworked, overwhelmed and depleted. When you feel as if you have no more to give authentically, everything is such a chore because you have given so much.

A Sign of The Times

I can remember a time when my husband and I were involved in an ongoing court battle regarding the utilization of the name of a history making band that he founded. This era of our lives was filled with so much uncertainty and more importantly, so much pain. To watch my husband be attacked so viciously and to be forced to fight for an entity that he created was unjust. As a wife, my role was to pour into my husband. As an attorney, my role was to consult and to fight on behalf of our family. Operating in both roles was draining, to say the least. And although I would operate in both roles at full capacity again in a heartbeat, doing so took a toll on me. There were times I felt burned out. The most catastrophic element of this scenario was that I was not aware of how depleted my emotional resources were. It wasn't until a random conversation with my girlfriend, that I realized that I couldn't offer anything of substance to the conversation. Me not being able to pour into her caused me concern. Over the years, I have always felt compelled and capable of giving encouragement to

those whom I come into contact with. Many refer to this as anointing. That special spark that influences and encourages people just wasn't there. I knew in that moment that I was burned out. I had no more to give and it was undeniable. I needed a break physically, mentally, and spiritually. What was most pressing was that I really needed to be poured into. No matter how strong you may be, it is not possible for you to pour from an empty pitcher.

Listen With Your Heart

The major problem that develops when you are approaching burnout is that everything becomes a chore, even the things that you most enjoy. You also tend to procrastinate, which sends other areas of your life into a tailspin simultaneously. It is possible that you become irritable and find yourself having to apologize for lack of patience or acting in exhaustion. I can recall being really tired of running, tired of reading, and tired of figuring out problems for myself and for others.

As women, we are created to pour into others, but you must ask yourself, who will pour into you? I had to step away, and my decision was to take some time off. I took a vacation to do nothing. I just wanted to exhale. I went to Guana. No one called me. I didn't have to fix a meal for anyone, and I didn't have to be accountable. The time away, although forced, taught me the power of recharging.

Today, I seek that same solace in going to the beach. I am a real Floridian beach goer. Even the drive to the beach is invigorating. The water, the sand, and the time to reconnect with God brings me back center. While at the beach, I spend time staring at the waves. On some occasions, I even take a long run to just let go. The ocean is a reminder that there is something bigger than each of us. This inspirational, directional time also allows me to engage in prayer. During those moments, I find myself trusting that God will give me the answers.

Press The Pause Button

To fully execute a recharge, you must also learn to press the pause button before you embark upon the most stressful moments of your life. For me, that means engaging in activities like going to the movies. Films that I don't have to think about such as *Beauty and*

the Beast or The Avenger series are most enjoyable for me. Pausing means giving yourself access to both levity and laughter. Laughter is indeed good for the soul. There is a direct parallel that can be drawn between entertainment and recharging. With the trying times that we live in, we cannot afford to not laugh. Laughter is healing. It's okay to regroup and restart. Taking time to laugh amidst a pause is an opportunity to look at what you're doing differently and to see the world around you differently.

Reflect and Refill with Purpose

If a pitcher is used to fill cups on a continual basis, then it will need to be refilled at some point in time. Consider your soul to be the pitcher. At all times, there is a space that needs to be refilled. This action of refilling can occur in a variety of ways. Taking time to read and expose yourself to positive content is another strategy that keeps you mentally aligned. Considering questions such as:

- What's the flow of my energy stream?
- What makes me feel replenished?
- What things seem to be consuming my energy?

These questions will allow you to recognize the ebbs and flows of your world and empower you with the skill set to deflect the things that steal your energy and embrace the things that replenish. Embrace my flow. It's okay to say no. Embracing your flow is listening to your internal instincts, and listening to what is right for you. Learning to trust and follow your gut positions you for success. I believe it to be a travesty when we don't admit that we need and deserve to recharge. Operating in this space does a disservice to the people you serve by not admitting you're in need of a refill. You were born with an internal GPS for a reason. Allow your soul to rest and enjoy the benefits of your ability to thrive.

Just Say No

When you recognize that time is your greatest resource, you will also discover that there is profound potential in saying no. There was a time when my goal was to literally be everything to everyone and on many days, I felt as though I had fallen short. My perspective has since changed. If you live long enough, you too will recognize that it is not humanly possible to be all things to all people. Even the most gracious will fail with this train of thinking. Setting specific and achievable goals and responsible limits on what can be achieved in a given time is a healthier option. If a task doesn't align with where I'm going or with my beliefs, it is a hard no for me.

When I was younger, I was more energy driven, today, I'm more purpose driven. Even in family settings and with friends, where it is my joy to serve, I have learned to say no where there is not time for me to be successful in the ask. Admittedly, saying no to family is more difficult. There are times that I wish I didn't have to deny requests but I would rather say no up front than to let someone down because I was unable to do what was asked of me. In retrospect, the main concern is we worry about hurting people's feelings. In the end, we must recognize that the feelings, emotional stability and well being that must first be considered is that of your own.

14 Ways to Practice Self-Care

Self-Care is the best care. The time that you take to care for yourself, will result in you being empowered to give your best self to the people, places and things that you care about most. Here are 14 of my go to strategies to engage in the priceless act of self-care:

- Engage in Quiet Time
- Take A Warm Bubble Bath
- Wake Up Early to Stretch
- Turn Off Your Phone
- Jog
- Eat a Healthy Snack
- Turn On the Music and Dance
- Burn A Scented Candle
- Cozy Under A Warm Blanket
- Garden
- Go For A Walk

- Do A Word Search
- Laugh
- Engage in a Cleansing Cry

SOUL

The Light

"Not one can dim the light that was divinely ordered."

-**Beryl McClary**-

Instead of conforming to the ways of the world and being affected by its messaging, reclaim your time, talent, and treasure. You have been ordained and divinely appointed to let the light that rests, rules and abides within you shine.

CHAPTER 10
SPIRITUALITY

There can be no profit if in the end you risk losing your soul.

-Beryl McClary-

I'm always communicating or speaking with my higher being, my Jesus. And while I recognize that many people have many different sources, Jesus is mine. He is an advisor and a restorer. It is possible to become separated from the source and during those moments, you are not plugged into the infinite power that we all have the power to access. This power, my spirituality is rooted in my Christian faith. I believe in the Bible and the word of God. That belief and the trust that I have been privileged to witness throughout my life remains unwavering, even in tough times. I respect other religions but I have a firm belief in my Christianity. If someone asks, "Why do you believe?" I reply, "Have you noticed that the sun never gets confused? It always rises on the east and sets on the west. The trees know where to root and where not to root." There has to be a being that is supreme for these things to exist.

Truth Must Be Personal

Thinking about God brings me unparalleled joy. It has been an awesome experience to believe in the word of God for myself. I share these sentiments with my children. My revelations and understanding of the words are based on my own study and being led by the inner spirit, which I call the Holy Spirit. There are teachings of others I don't agree with and I don't accept them as my truths. I believe that spirituality is based upon a personal relationship with the greater one. My personal spiritual goal is to remain attuned with God and his calling on my life. Nothing is impossible with God. Blessed is he who believes. It is because of my belief and God's grace that I know that

I can achieve every goal and every dream that my mind can conceive and if it is in God's perfect will. If I keep those big dreams in front of me, my God, my Jesus, my Holy Spirit will get me to that point. It is comforting to know that I do not have to depend solely on my limited skills or limited knowledge or skill set. Lead me to things that are bigger than me.

Word of Sovereignty

As a voracious reader, I spend a great deal of time engaged in the self-help genre. There are no limits placed on what type of content that I consume, I believe that in words, there lies value and vast possibilities. As I ponder all that I have read, it is still my belief that the desire to want, be and to do our best is still rooted in biblical principles. No matter how many gurus share their systems and concepts for greatness, the simplistic principles of the Bible are still the common theme even if not referenced as such. We never read about the wealthy and their habits. Even though they don't quote biblical scriptures, the gurus of past and present speak to the power of manifestation, which equally qualifies as the exercise of faith. The words that are placed atop pages that encourage you to believe in yourself and to chase your dreams, are shining examples of the mustard seed principle. If we dare to exercise faith that is the size of a mustard seed, then we shall have divine permission to reap harvest. What greater promise can we ask for? No matter who reproduces it or how many times we read a promise of faith revised, God's word alone is sovereign.

Discipleship

My religion is not outside of me, nor is it something that I do. My faith, religion and spirituality is who I am. The love of God has allowed me to know that I am whole and to freely exercise compassion toward others. And even amidst all of the compassion, there are still moments of life that God makes you endure. It is my belief that endurance enables you to forgive. By walking in the mighty grace of the Lord, you understand the power of forgiveness because you find yourself in need of it. When you are a believer in Jesus, you can let go of bitterness and forgive those who trespass against you. Our family has been under personal attack and what felt like persecution amidst the countless court battles with my husband's former band mater. His only goal was to work and be a provider for his family. It is hard to extend grace when you know that there are people who desire to take food away from the mouths of your children. There were many days that I prayed to God and asked what it was that we were to learn from all that transpired? Those tumultuous times taught every member of our family that our hope rests in God. We kept smiles on our faces and the children never missed a beat, even though there were days that we wondered how it would all get done. That same hope that grew on the inside and manifested in love and kindness on the outside was the best example of discipleship. Church, religion, spirituality and the exercise thereof does not always mean confinement to four walls. When we give our best to others and show up with a kind heart, we are disciples and our actions are purposed to make the world a better place.

Stand for Something

Spirituality is not something that can be forced upon people, even though tradition and society at large has attempted to do so. My life has allowed me to recognize that how I show up in the world may be the only example that another person that I come into contact may see of God. People will learn more about what I stand for by who I am, than what I say. Even my children are allowed to interpret God's love for themselves. We encourage them to evolve in alignment with their experiences. Although heartbreaking, we have all witnessed our share of hypocrites and those whose actions were polar opposite the doctrines that they outwardly subscribed to. From world leaders to spiritual confidants, abuse of power is real, which is why I don't take the opportunities presented to me to share God's love lightly. What I do know is that life is too hard to believe in nothing. There is so much of what we experience that doesn't make sense to the human realm of possibilities. Much of what we will live through can only be understood in the spiritual realm.

It is my continuous prayer that my children will experience the will of God. I have always known God's grace and was fortunate to witness it at various magnitudes throughout my life. My Graves' Disease diagnosis in law school was at times too much to bear. My condition had become so severe that my eyes started to change. I was left with one healthy eye after treatment. The eye that was most affected protruded and those who I would encounter assumed that I was born like that. I looked like I was startled all the time. Even though the eye healed after treatment, the eyelid had thickened and put immense pressure on the eye. I felt so disfigured. I thought I looked like a gargoyle. Being born again and standing firmly in grace, I chose to keep fighting in pursuit of graduation. For almost two years, I sat at what felt like never ending doctor's appointments. While there, I would repeat, *Lord, I have asked for my eye to go back into place. Have you seen my eye?* In those moments, I was pleading with him for mercy. My plea wasn't pretty but it didn't have to be. I knew that God would take me as I was. Then one day I looked in the mirror and my eye was back to normal. There was no warning or series of eens that indicated that my eye would be restored. Looking in the mirror, I started to shout. God loved me enough to hold on to my word and to honor my requests. For this and many other reasons, I stand firmly on his word.

Prayer is Power

After graduating from law school, I was thrilled to have made it over what I thought to be some of the hardest days of my life. Little did I know, I would need to harness the power of prayer to get me and many others through trying times on the horizon. I found myself in the thick of it, practicing law for equality and justice for all. Some of the more superficial arguments in the courtroom were not my cup of tea. I demanded justice, especially for the unjust treatment of African-American people. In the '80s, the sentences were very severe for black men, some wrongly or should I say many, wrongly accused. Being on the front lines taught me a great deal but the most powerful lesson was discovered in prayer. After watching judges who were ready, willing and able to give maximum penalties, changing lives and legacies, I knew that it would take more than being smart and excelling in law school to combat the warfare. Albeit, some of those represented in courts came from broken homes and others were products of socioeconomic hardship that led to alternative methods of survival. And then there were those who fell victim to the contrived narrative delivered by a history riddled with inequality. These levels of prejudice could only be fought with prayer. I would pray for my clients as if they were my own children. I prayed for strategies to deliver while on trial and for insight and wisdom to see the things that I could not. No matter what internal messaging is force fed, whether true or untrue, nothing can come between the power of prayer when the person on her knees is intentional. The power of prayer never returns void.

Not only did I pray in the courtroom, but I also prayed for divine guidance and intervention when raising my children. I gave thanks unto God for having sent and approved of a loving husband. For well over years, I had ample opportunities to marry someone else, but I did not. Glory be to God. As women, we don't always know if we are dating or devoting our time to the right person or who

God selects for us. In my adult life, patience truly became a virtue, because I submitted myself to the God I believed in and I knew he was good. This patience allowed me to wait for a mate that was hand selected for me. And I must admit that the packaging was not what I had anticipated. When I met my dear husband, he was engaged to someone else. We were both engaged in community work and endeavoured to make an impact in the lives of others. As fate would have it, through the grapevine, I had heard that his relationship ended and that he had become a Christian. It was in this spirit and awareness that wrote him a letter inviting him to church. Little did I know that same patience that I mentioned would be put to the test. My letter was not responded to or even acknowledged until some two years later. Out of what felt like the blue, he called me and said he was responding to my letter and that he wanted to meet up with me. Although the meeting happened, our time together was short lived as he would eventually return to California, amidst his musical career endeavours. We remained in touch but I can't say that I knew for sure how it would all manifest. Upon his return, he asked me to be his wife and I was delighted. Today, we celebrate 27 years of marriage. I don't question whether or not the marriage was ordained by God, it was a blessed affair. My wedding song was to Glory to God because I wanted to honor him with the union that he blessed me to realize. Everything that I could have asked or wished for came to fruition amidst our union. My brother, who had also been jailed prior to the wedding was able to get out to be in the ceremony and my heart was full. With prayer, God can bless any situation.

With every passing year of my life, I have found solace and inspiration in taking steps with God. I am never alone because I hold on to his promises and they have kept me. The scriptures in the Bible give me something to hold on to. I will fear no evil because thou are with me. On more occasions than I can remember, I shared this sentiment with my children.

They witnessed faith because we resolved to walk in it. It is my belief that the Bible is better seen than read. Faith and trust remind you to be the last man standing, even when the storms are raging. We must all learn to ask ourselves if our faith is enough to stand when the world around us appears to be caving in? When we trust God, some way he will calm the seas and bring the most tumultuous moments of our lives to pass. Whatever you have to endure, whatever your cross to bear, it has been assigned to you because God has equipped you with what you need to triumph. No one can stand for you. No one can bleed for you. If you believe unwaveringly, you have access to all power. It is with my heart that I know that our beloved children will be an example of God's goodness, and it is my solemn prayer that the legacy that we leave behind speaks of grace and mercy forever.

14 Days of Self-Reflection

We learn most not from experience, but time spent reflecting upon experience.

-Beryl McClary-

One of the most important things that you can do to grow spiritually is to reflect upon your life and the moments, people and experiences that shape who you are. I invite you to spend the next 14 days journaling and allowing your spirit to speak truth.

Day 1: What things are you most grateful for:

Day 2: What things are you most proud of:

Day 3: What does spirituality mean to you:

Day 4: What do you believe your purpose to be:

Day 5: Who are your favorite people to be with:

Day 6: What calms your soul:

Day 7: What are your fears:

Day 8: What makes you happy:

Day 9: What makes you lose track of time:

Day 10: What are words that bring you peace:

Day 11: How do you define unconditional love:

Day 12: What do you wish others knew about you:

Day 13: What moves you to tears:

Day 14: How do you want to grow spiritually:

CHAPTER 11
RELATIONSHIPS

Companionship must not be optional, for life was never meant to be lived alone.

-Beryl McClary-

There are only two things that we must remember to win at love, and they are as follows:

1. Love is patient.
2. Love is kind.

If we held these two truths in high esteem, love gives us more than our hearts could ever desire. In many ways we make love complicated, but it is far more simple than we give the concept credit for. Love is about how we treat others and not about what we look to receive. We have no way to control the way that others love, but we maintain autonomy over ourselves.

For many reasons, I've always been drawn to love. Even when reading the scriptures, I am reminded of the love from which we were crafted. God drew us with a court of love. Likewise we have to be kept in a court of love.

Loyalty and unconditional love are important.

Love & Marriage

Nestled under the umbrella of God's love is the love I share with my husband, Thomas. After having been married for several years, I recognize now more than ever how important it is that we get married for the right reasons. Before finding the man that God created for me, I used to pray to God asking, "How much longer?"

While in college I dated a much older man. He was a graduate of Harvard, but also a philanderer. All through my college years he treated me well, and I prayed about our relationship's longevity. His wayward intentions prevented me from continuing our relationship. Admittedly, I was heartbroken but yielding to God's will. Thirty-five years later I learned that he committed suicide. It was tragic. Through it all, I learned that the love that is meant for you will never escape you. Anyone that God does not select for you, you must find the strength to mark *Return to Sender*.

Marriage was something that I saw for myself and wished deeply for, but I would not be honored with this gift until God said so. And even though I desperately wanted to be married, I know that it must be ordained and divinely aligned. Do not get married because you feel pressured or because everyone else is doing it. These are shallow thrills that may lack substance in the future. Learn to live your life to the fullest so that love without limits can discover you. Finding *the one* is no easy feat, but there are some indicators that help you to just know. I knew that I didn't want anyone who didn't have a good sense of humor. With my husband, even his eyes laugh. We've learned not to take things so seriously. This is one of the most powerful ways to keep the marriage light and healthy. Beyond love, there must be the presence of commitment. When things are difficult, as they will sometimes be, you must remember why you got married. That brightness in the eyes, that quick smile, that gentleness, has the power to bring you back center. Time together also serves as a reminder that you don't have the power to change another person. Don't even try to make your significant other into the person you want them to be. Learning to respect the differences and taking time to learn, appreciate and to communicate about them is key.

Watch how you say things and learn to accept gentle, yet constructive criticisms. You need someone to tell you that the dress is too tight or the pants are too old, but it should be mutual, not one-sided. There should be commonality in your goals, and a lot of love. Learning to exchange love can result in a plentiful exchange. I love when my husband tells me I look pretty. I immediately tell him how handsome he is. Marriage is about lifting each other up. Try to avoid criticizing. It's not going to motivate them or you. Marriage requires a lot of prayer and the ability to forgive and forget. A good marriage benefits from forgiveness and forgetting. A lot of *pay it no mind* goes a long way.

I can remember a time that I was counseling a young lady who had developed a wedge between her and her husband. It was something small but they were holding their ground. My advice was for her to avoid leveraging the shut down and silent treatment. That's not a good strategy for a relationship. It's not a good substitute for authentic communication. When uncovered, it's a passive aggressive manipulation that denotes...If you don't do what I want you to do, then I won't speak to you. Love can't breathe in spaces like this, it is suffocated. Sometimes you have to schedule a time to talk.. Maybe a little after things calm down. With a little time to think things over and for your heart to settle, you might discover that it wasn't what they were trying to communicate. And as difficult as it may be, you need to talk. Understand that you need to find resolutions and commonality. At least take the time to gain understanding. Never forget that it's okay to have an opinion without being right. Understand that some things are not worth it.

Learn and lead with kindness. Good sexual intimacy in a marriage comes from being kind. Withholding sex as a weapon does not lead to healthy exchanges. Push notions of perfection into afterthoughts. The best love arises through imperfection. In kindness, you are empowered to pick and choose your fights, while keeping everyone's best interests in mind. When you know confidently that your partner has your back, then you can feel safe in rendering kindness, even when at odds. No matter what has happened, I have always known throughout our 27 years that Thomas has loved me, and I relaxed in that love. He has always known that I loved him as well. This exchange provided for an endurance that neither of us could have imagined or planned for, even if we tried. Love and respect for one another must also be by products of kindness. A man wants respect. Don't marry someone that you are not able to respect. One of the ways we show that love and respect is to stop what you're doing and give them your attention. Look in their face and hear what they're trying to say. If we can remember that love is patient and love is kind, then we can discover an open door to bask in the glory of love and marriage.

A Mother's Love

The love exchanged between my husband Thomas and I flowed over into our children. I knew that I was smitten the moment I chose to raise my children over ascension in the career I had fought so hard for. As professional women who wear ambition on our sleeves, we want recognition for the goals that we relentlessly pursue and conquer. Much of the chase requires being a part of the networking society and cultivating professional relationships. There were times that I thought I should be progressing more professionally, and times that I believed that I should have more speaking engagements, and more responsibilities at the firm. I chose to be the best mom that I could be and to pour into my children all that was necessary to make them strong and healthy.

When the children were first born, I can recall enlisting help from a nanny. Over time I learned that as much as I wanted help, I also wanted the influence in my children's lives to be me. I needed to know what was being said and how their souls were cared for. It was not my preference to have someone else form them. If I did not assume ownership for speaking life into them when they were little, who could I expect to do it? I wanted them to be happy but I also wanted them to be courageous and not be defined by societal imposed standards.

To be the best mother that I could be and to ensure my presence in my children's lives, I learned to say no professionally. There were times that I couldn't work during the Saturday meetings or remain in team briefings that lasted until late hours at night. Although my children didn't go to daycare, I was not a stay at home mother. My ambition pushed me to give my best attempt at managing it all. My only desire was to not feel guilty about having made decisions that I felt were in the best interest of my family as well as my professional goals and objectives.

As a working mother, I would maintain consistent hours for work and consistent hours at home with the children. When at home, I still had projects to do for work, but my children took precedence over any desire to be successful. The power of no was something that had to be considered when raising children and in consideration of matters of the heart.

With the rendering of love, also came taking the time to get to know each of our children. Knowing your child is very important. One of my boys was kind of quiet. I spoke with him and found out he'd been teased at school for stuttering, so he chose to be quiet. I remember that my stuttering was something that my father dealt with and he too was a quiet man. I continued to instill courage and skills to navigate moments when the world was unkind. I spent lots of time reminding everyone that they were loved in our home, and although the world would not always be kind, home was a safe space to which they could retreat.

Beyond love, it also takes courage to be a mom. My prayer for mothers is that we each recognize our own strength and never forget how to channel the power of love to propel you through.

And although the world was not always kind, the years were good to us. In our home, we often spoke about love and admiration. Our goal was to ensure that everyone felt, heard and saw that they were both loved and appreciated. The greatest testament to this was the year that our kids wanted us to have a romantic anniversary. They were all so young, but old enough to make plans. They called around

to various relatives to learn to cook a meal. They took the time to prepare my favorite salad, set the table with candles, and pretended to be the staff of a restaurant while serving our food. They encouraged us to dance and the laughter was never ending. It was such an act of love. They were mirrors to the light of love that we had been working so hard to ensure they felt in our home.

Love in the Workplace

The best advice that I can give for work relationships is to do the work. I always tell young people that they are not there to change the world, they are there to do the work and follow instructions. Many mistake work for a place of socialization, and it demeans the integrity of why everyone has been positioned there. I am a firm believer in doing your work and doing it well. The truth that many will not admit is that there is a lot of treachery in the workplace. Some smiling faces aren't really smiling. Work is to give you experience in a particular area. Don't take it personally. Don't let it define your acceptance or your lack thereof. Always assume everybody loves you and love everybody. Don't put yourself in the predicament of being too vocal.

A Friend Indeed

I have friends that I've maintained relationships with since kindergarten. We're constantly in contact. I know about their children and their pets. We're involved with each other's lives and we nurture our relationships with constant love. The love that I speak of looks different for each one of us. You can't maintain a relationship if you're not reaching out. Spending time counting how many times someone reached out to you versus how many times you have reached out to them and allowing that to determine if or when you will reach out next is unhealthy. To have a good friend you have to be one. No one wants a bellyaching friend. Lose count and stay in contact by any means necessary. Be genuinely interested in their lives. Send a joke or two to keep the laughter alive. To maintain long term relationships, there needs to be love. I have another friend who is very different from me, but she's always been trustworthy. Although our approaches to life are very different, we've found commonality. We have taken vacations together. I was with her on her first plane trip. She was so afraid, and she kept looking up at the ceiling of the plane. By the time we took that trip, I had visited other countries, and flown several times, but none of that mattered. My only goal was to help her feel calm in the moment. Life unfortunately takes us on different roads and winding paths, and she eventually battled with significant health concerns. Through it all, we are still good friends and we talk about the dreams we had thirty years ago. I've always kept my close friends close to me. No matter the circumstances, we are truthful and understanding.

Lessons in Love

Attempting to love has been one of my greatest teachers. The invaluable sentiments that I learned on a quest to love have managed to stick with me, and amidst these pages, I share them with you.

- **Love is work.** Loving will not always be easy, but worth it.
- **Be Quiet and Listen.** Stay quiet and don't become argumentative because there might be a fault in your understanding. Learn to disagree without being disagreeable. No one has to be right.
- **It is Free to Concede.** If it doesn't mean that there is something to be lost personally, then consider a different type of position at that point. There is always the option to be quiet and walk away peacefully, or to choose to resume the call at a later date. In the grand scheme of things, it's not going to make a difference.
- **Results Matter.** You don't change anybody's mind by being argumentative. Simply being personable or even becoming a little more compassionate makes a difference. Evaluate the situation and make a determination. Consider what you want the end result to be? Most importantly, consider your motives and if your actions are rooted in love. In the end, the only thing that will matter is how you chose to live, and how you chose to love.

The Relationship Checklist

The give and take of relationships is what makes being in one special. Here's a checklist that I often use to monitor the health of my relationships.

Ask Yourself?	YES	NO	IN PROGRESS
Can I Love with No Conditions?			
Am I Willing to Exchange Power?			
Do I See Growth and Progress?			
Is There An Exchange of Continuous Support?			

CHAPTER 12
TRAVEL

Those who wander are not lost, they are found.

-Beryl McClary-

It was always my heart's desire to see the world. My friends from college were from all over the world including India, South America, and Africa. The cultivation of these relationships were a clear indication to me that there was more to see beyond our borders. Communism was still in effect and dictatorships were still around, but I didn't allow that to limit what I saw to be possible for me to see. In college, I made it my goal to learn about how world affairs were oriented, which piqued my academic interests. The only solution to address my yearning for learning about foreign soil was to go see it for myself.

Shortly after college, I began practicing law and serving as a missionary. My initial travel was to countries nearby before truly venturing out. The feel of the sunlight from an atmosphere that I had never witnessed and the breeze of the wind in my hair in the open air made me feel close to God. With my soul overflowing from bearing witness to all that God had managed to create, I was also able to understand things I had seen in the Bible. Seeing the world gives you a different view of life. And you see the integration of people's history. Often, I would make it a point to learn about the country before I visited.

My first large scale mission trip was to Peru. Prior to going, I had never seen mountains or deserts. We were assigned to pray for the people who lived there and to commune with them, while introducing them to Christ. In the early 80's, most people had seen only white missionaries traditionally. There I was, a girl from a small town in Florida, praying for people who had never been in close proximity to someone like me, nor had I met them. They were beautiful people and it was my honor to be of service. Not only did I learn much about the people, but also the terrain was something I had not witnessed.

There were mud huts and mansions. Learning to be gracious and answer questions while working to hear of their concerns was what we had been called to do. We not only worked with the adults but also took care of the orphans.

Not all of the moments were sweet. There were some native people who did not like Americans. They often expected Americans to be very cocky and arrogant and in some instances, they were correct. Even the Gospel can be presented as the American way if not curated for the people to whom you speak. You had to be careful with your delivery and learn to appreciate the small things and the people. Taking time to ensure that you are not belittling but admiring. Learning to not see things from the perspective of an American, but from the perspective of those you shared the gospel with was key.

The most memorable trip I took was to Israel. One of the tour guides fought in the war of 1989 when the Jews declared it as their homeland. He was so wonderful and pleasant. We talked a lot about the political atmosphere of Israel and what I had learned about Jews. He came back with a gift bearing my name written in Hebrew. After we left the VMC, we went to the Masada Plateau in the east where the Israelis lived. It was interesting to walk through it and see where they had developed running water in the desert. There was a war and the Israelites fought on high land with the more numerous opponents on the lowland. They fought to the end but were eventually overcome. They hid people in the waters and they survived to tell the story. That was memorable for me that people at this location knew the enemy were numerous and they knew that they were going to die. Their stories demonstrated the tenacity of a people. I was also blessed to see Russia when the wall went down, which further added to my repertoire of memories and perspectives that we live in a wondrous world. My travels also taught me that we must not limit ourselves, for the possibilities of who and what we can become are limitless.

He's Got The Whole World in His Hands

As a result of my experiences abroad, my priorities changed. I eliminated the things that were not important in the whole scheme of life. I did that for many years, enjoying the different countries and people, and when life transitioned me into a wife and a mother, I resolved to make sure that my family had the opportunity to see the world for themselves. When the children were young, we took them on a mission trip to Honduras. As I recall, it was a rainy season and there was not good drainage, which made for a muddy trip. We were housed at an orphanage run by Americans and it was very nice.

The greatest gift on that trip was working to provide housing to the elderly, many of whom had been left outside to die. They built huts using a mold and filled them with mud. There was no plumbing, so the floors of the homes would often be muddy.

When the children returned that year, I could see the unraveling wonder in their eyes. They started to understand why at Christmas we would sponsor a mission trip for other families. They didn't ask for much, because they recognized that they were blessed. They understood that material things didn't make the biggest difference in life.

I continued to take them on mission trips to broaden their horizons. Although I had never been much of a tourist, it had always been my practice to see the area and take a tour of the areas that revealed the true culture of the land and to learn the history of the place. The children would get so agitated because I would make them read to understand our reason for being on the trip and to understand how they could be impactful. I knew that one day, it would expand their horizons and provide them with a worldly view. Later in life, I knew that they would understand that their travel around the world and research about their travel would broaden their scope. One of the most beautiful places that we went to was Vancouver, Canada. It was a marvelous, marvelous sight. We also went to the rainforest together and that was a memorable experience.

There was another time when Thomas was in Switzerland. One man came and met my husband with all of his albums in hand. He told him all about his history, and how much of a fan he was. He asked only for one of his guitar picks. That was pretty cool.

From preaching at the prisons to praying in the mud huts, my children have seen me serve all over the world. I would not trade the experience of seeing the world with them for anything in the world. I encourage every mother and father to take your children to see the world. It must be placed at the forefront of your goals. There is immense value in seeing the world that will inevitably increase the quality of life.

There's No Place Like Home

Adventure has always been a part of my personality. I never wanted to sit idle. My travels have left me to only be grateful for the privilege of seeing and doing. Professionally, I was afforded opportunities to stay with diplomats and the attorneys for the UN. As a criminal defense attorney, I watched lawyering in other countries, and garnered an appreciation of America. And as much as I recognize it as a blessing to travel, I am always appreciative to be back on the soil that I call home. There is no country without flaw but I am thankful for the myriad of choices that we have in the United States. Admittedly our justice system demonstrates an undeniable difference between how white people and black people are treated, but America is where we chose to call home. It is the enhanced perspective that gives me comfort in knowing that the world has more to offer each of us. The more you get out and see, touch, and hear from the world, the more life and the prospect of promise and notions of what could be, embrace you back.

CHAPTER 13
MONEY

Making money is one thing, creating wealth is another. The goal must be able to establish financial freedom for generations to come.

-**Beryl McClary**-

In consideration of finances, I tend to be conservative. As a mother of six children, I tend budget conscious. The greatest lesson that I learned about money is that it is always present. Regardless of what is happening in your personal finances or around you, money exists somewhere. The goal is to locate if for yourself and to determine the best ways to multiply it to create abundance for yourself and your family and to give to the world. Taking time to acquire education on the best strategies for leveraging financial freedom has always been of importance to me. If you are not open to learning, then money will not flow freely to you.

Mind Over Matter

Growing up in a middle class home, also meant that we used the money that we had to care for our immediate needs. As an adult, I began to learn the importance of passive income. To further educate myself, I enrolled in a class. Our ability to create various streams of income will always prove to be valuable. There is not a time when we do not need to harness the power of passive income to be working for us while we are asleep.

We have to be mindful of where we are in life and where we want to go such that we can calculate our finances and needs accordingly. It takes discipline to make money and even more gumption to keep money. Discovering the determination to exercise self-control on a daily basis is also a part of keeping our money in motion. When we learn to do without things that are expendable, we also learn to discover the things that are of most value. A consistent quest to ask ourselves how we can increase our value in the workplace, as entrepreneurs, as side hustlers, in the boardrooms and even amongst our friends and family is an act of great power. When we increase our value, we in turn increase our wealth. The traditional educational system does not teach us to think in terms of increasing our incomes by increasing the value that we can offer to the world in a specific sector. If a child grows up in a home with parents who are financially savvy, this could mean that they are not exposed to best financial literacy practices, thus creating a deficit. Although I wasn't taught about finances, I made up my mind to not allow this factor to be a part of what the outcome would be. The more that we learn about money and the various ways to generate more of it, we must make it a point to share it with future generations so that they can avoid many of the costly mistakes that have been made and advance themselves and their families.

The Balancing Act

The money that you gain and the money that you keep depends on your personality and attitudes towards finances. My personality is such that I don't like to part with money. On so many occasions, my disposition drove my husband nuts. There were times that he wanted to make purchases for the house or for the children, but all I wanted to do was to save money. I would of course bend on necessities, but being frugal is in my DNA. There are levels of extreme when it comes to finances, and I'd like to say that I fall somewhere in the middle. I had an aunt on my mother's side who was so frugal that she would lay paper towels that were only moist out to dry so that they could be reused for minor spills. That's one extreme, and I don't believe that I have reached that level of severity, but only time will tell. There has to be a balance between enjoying life and maintaining control to keep your livelihood intact. Experience is also a graceful teacher. There were times that I made the budget too rigid, and from those experiences, I discovered loopholes and gaps to be filled.

Set the Goal, Chase the Vision

Self-control is more attainable when you are chasing specific financial goals. Breaking down your financial landscape into quarters is a powerful way to quantify the amount of time that you have to invest in a goal and to make the actions that you need to take towards the accomplishment of the goal more clear.

If you were to sit down right now to make a list of three financial goals that you want to achieve those goals would become real. If you went as far as to write down a date that those goals should be accomplished by, you would now be accountable for those goals. If you resolved to check that list periodically to chart how far you have come and how far you still need to go, then you would have a bonafide plan. To take things a step farther, consider taking the large goals and breaking them down into steps and taping that list of steps on a wall or a desk that you frequent most often. If you keep your goals in front of you, then you will position yourself for a win. As an attorney, I strategize completing a certain number of cases in a six month period. This exercise allowed my heart, mind, and soul to work on an answering to that goal. Although we do know that things are not always on time, taking accountability for the things that will manifest in our financial lives is half the battle. Sometimes you have to dream again and recognize that you are worthy of more than what you see directly in front of you. As we get older and we've been knocked down, financially we stop dreaming. We must never stop believing that our brightest days are ahead and that the universe has more abundance to offer us. Even in our finances, the impossible is possible.

Self Education on finances

I am an avid reader and learner . Taking responsibility for my own financial goals , I would read and take webinars to discover other means of acquiring income. These webinars included learning how to invest in stock, and real estate.. I was also abreast of the trends in technology and the world of digital products and stores. The learning curve is a little steep . But, I was willing to obtain and receive coaching and become a part of groups that which could break down the new strategies and assist in the implementation of them. Jim Rohn, was an influencer who died said to increase your income you must increase your value. Education will get you a job but, self education will make you rich. This was a quote I never forgot and impacted my thinking greatly. If each person has 24 hours in a day and one person makes an hourly wage of $20 and the executive at Disney gets a salary of and an annual bonus of $10 million , , what made the difference in income? It was the value each person brings in solving problems.

This resulted in an epiphany that I needed to change and acquire new skill for the market place. Learning is always but action is what gets results. Immediate action executing what was learned.

am an avid reader and learner . Taking responsibility for my own financial goals , I would read and take webinars to discover other means of acquiring income. These webinars included learning how to invest in stock, and real estate.. I wa also abreast of the trends in technology and the world of digital products and stores. The learning curve is a little steep . But, I was willing to obtain and receive coaching and become a part of groups that which could break down the new strategies and assist in the implementation of them. Jim Rohn, was an influencer who died said to increase your income you must increase your value. Education will get you a job but, self education will make you rich. This was a quote I never forgot and impacted my thinking greatly. If each person has 24 hours in a day and one person makes an hourly wage of $20 and the executive at Disney gets a salary of and an annual bonus of $10 million , , what made the difference in income? It was the value each person brings in solving problems.

This resulted in an epiphany that I needed to change and acquire new skill for the market place. Learning is always but action is what gets results. Immediate action executing what was learned.

CHAPTER 14
DISCOVERING PURPOSE

The mystery of the human experience is discovering purpose. Life is what we do to figure it out.

-**Beryl McClary**-

A question we all ask is what are we here for? Is life more than this job that I don't like, or the day to day routine that I am fed up with executing? We are put on this earth to serve. I knew that service was my passion, and I discovered my ability to render service through law. My purpose was to do the best I could to represent each of my clients. I was concerned that they would be treated fairly in the judicial system. So often I would see disparity. When I sat in the audience of the courtroom, I was reminded of why I became a defense attorney. When judges were handing out sentences like candy on Halloween to these young African American boys, my heart broke. At the time, what I struggled to translate the passion that I felt in my heart into money. And even though there was more money to be made in other practices, I always knew that I was meant to be a defense attorney. The other areas of practice did not move me, and tug on my heart to exercise extreme levels of compassion. It was in this space that purpose was defined.

Purpose is An Individual Sport

It is difficult to work or do something that you are not passionate about. You have to ask yourself what you genuinely love and desire to do? You have to analyze and examine what comes easy for you. Train on the things that you are good at, and seek to improve over time. I recall meeting a young lady who was a secretary for a defense attorney. Her husband had been convicted of manslaughter, and they had one child together. When we met, she was in her late 20s, early 30s, and the weight of everything evolving in her life was trying. Amidst our talks, I encouraged her to keep going to school and to move towards obtaining a law degree. It is possible to be 40 with a law degree or 40 without. In this case, the goal was still the goal. She started taking classes, and pushing through the obstacles of her life to achieve her goals. Although things did not work out with her first husband, she remained steadfast in her motherhood and the pursuit of her education. Eventually she remarried and approximately ten years later, by the age of 40, she too became a lawyer. We can all agree that time will not stop, and we must allow it to serve as motivation to do what we desire to do in life, regardless of circumstance.

Desires of the Heart

When in search of purpose, you must learn to lighten your heart from the burdens of the world and to listen to your heart. And when you have become wise enough to listen, learn to follow your heart. There are times where I engaged in opportunities that were not in my heart, and they didn't serve me well. You have to have a greater reason to do whatever it is that you dedicate your time to doing. Always ask yourself why are you doing what you're doing? Never cease to question your motives, as they will give you the answers that you need and desire.

Whatever you do, do your best. One day, your life experiences will be used by others who desire to push forward. Even when you are not aware of it, you are someone's reason to not give up. More importantly, you are your reason to not give up. As sure as you awake each day, you awake with purpose.

For as many years as I can remember, my family was my why. I kept a series of photos of my children nearby on my desk. Seeing their faces reminded me that they looked to us for provision. On days that I didn't feel like moving, the looks on their faces made me do it anyway. Seeing them happy and cared for was the joy of my heart. I also recognized that I had the power to teach them what it meant to be successful.

When things would become overwhelming, I channeled my passion, which was being a provider and a caregiver. For me, then, nurturing was my purpose and my calling. From the livingroom to the courtroom, I found great value in watching those that I had been assigned to fight for thrive.

Past. Present. Future.

Whether you know it or not, your present is preparation for your future. As your life evolves, the matter of your heart evolves. For me, that meant watching the children grow up and become independent. The onset of a new era of life, also meant that my personal and professional dreams evolved outside of the courtroom. I found myself desiring to inspire and empower women who were beginning the challenges that I had once weathered as a professional with a family. I found myself desiring to establish more of a presence in civic organizations in my community. My heart, mind, and soul began to dream again after the notion of the children being fully dependent on me evolved. It is my belief that we should all seek a new dream at various junctures in our lives. It's certainly scary to redefine or to expand your dreams and purpose, but always worth it. Evolve often. You can conquer your dreams, if you are willing to take action.

Why Not You?

Be advised, people will always encourage you to pursue an occupation whether you like it or not because it will earn you a living. People will tell you to follow the tried and true pattern to have a good job with three weeks of vacation. They will encourage you to collect your check every two weeks and to build your retirement. And all of these things are a way to make a living, until they don't feel like fun anymore. No one talks about the moment when you realize that your normal life is in need of a purpose filled upgrade. And because no one speaks about it, the path to the pursuit of your purpose outside of what society has dedicated that you be and do can be lonely and confusing. In many instances, some never pursue purpose outside of the norm because of the fear.

Fear in the face of new purpose and passion can come in the form of feeling as though you are too old to try something new. Fear can come in the form of adversity and learning curves because the times have changed. Fear can come in the form of retreat to your new goals leading to complacency and comfort in continuing to do life as you have always known it.

Amidst one of my moments in preparation for a life pivot, I was reading a book about breaking into an industry. During the Second World War, there was a man who was determined not to die in the gas chamber. He devised a plan. He didn't desire to survive. He desired to get out. He laid with corpses for a week. When they went to dump those bodies into a mass hole, he stood up amidst the dead bodies and started running. He kept running. He was determined to live and not die. To pursue a new purpose, you must be determined to live and not die.

You Can Be Many Things

Don't be discouraged because you desire to do many things. There are lawyers who are cardiologists. Maya Angelou was many things. She was a dancer, she was a poet, and she was a writer. She lived life and traveled. Not only can you reinvent and recreate, you can add to your life because you are multidimensional. We have been taught to be focused on one thing, but in your next chapter that is not the case. If you can see something different, even if it's reading a new genre of book, then do it. You are called for more.

After lawyering for so many years, I found myself at a crossroads. Now, in my 60s, I too have asked the questions… What's my passion? Why have I been placed on this earth? What work should I be doing? I had to evaluate because the answers of the past had now evolved into new responses.

How then do you arrive at these answers? How do you know when life is asking you to write a new chapter? It's on the inside. It's the dream that keeps waking you up at night. It's the thing that you can't stop thinking about.

If you decide to write your next chapter, you must remember that it takes courage. No one will make it easy for you or give you an opportunity to pursue your dreams, it will be left up to you. No one cares more about you than you. Who do you really want to be? Does this line up with where you want to go? The older you are, the less time you have for failing to take action. Decide where you want to go. And visualize so you know where you're going. If your heart desires, then set it on fire.

Write The Vision. Make It Plain.

Writing your next chapter is about resolving to be the best you that you can be. What would you do if you knew that you would not fail? Write it down. Write down your strengths and talents and what you're naturally interested in. What would your ideal life look like? How can you express yourself to serve others and to make the world better? Is it painting? Is it through song? Write these things down. Your answers need not be long, only intentional.

What would your life be if you had no impediments? Use your inner guidance. You are far more powerful than you know. Examination of these things can lead you to your purpose. You will have a clearer picture of who you are.

With clarity, you will find that life will bring opportunities and experiences to you, but you must not wait, you must pursue. God or the universe will be attracted to you when you've reached clarity. Keep walking. Keep writing.

EPILOGUE

The goal must always be to give the world the best of you, not what is left of you.

-Beryl McClary

You are one choice away from the life that you have always dreamed of living. The deciding factor will be your exercise of courage. I have a burning desire to live before I die and it is my prayer that I have encouraged you to share in this sentiment with me. There is no time like the present. Today is the day that you must resolve to seize. This moment will never come again. Always remember that the present is yours for the taking.

You must resolve to be a lifelong learner, and to set goals so big that they scare you just a little. You must craft a plan to achieve your goals, and you must fight to ensure that the requirements of daily life don't get in the way. Acquire new knowledge, discover and engage with new networks, and reward yourself for small wins. This moment, this life, belongs to you. Live your life to the fullest capacity. Chase the life you want relentlessly. Opportunity is yours for the taking. It is with these sentiments that you have the power to write The Next Chapter.

CLOSING SENTIMENTS

She who rules her mind rules her world.

-Beryl McClary-

Simply put, be who you would like to be. Trust that you have everything that you need inside of you. There will always be life going on around you; take care to discover yourself amidst the chaos. If ever you find yourself confused, stop and exhale. Find out what your strengths are. And be accepting that others may not accept you as you are. Also put forth just as much effort to be accepting of others. If you find yourself being critical, this could mean that you are too busy bringing others down to figure yourself out. Be open to change and listen to your gut. Walk in love.

"Decide what kind of life you want to live, and take action to live it."

Beryl McClary

ABOUT THE AUTHOR

Authentic Determination

With a legal career spanning more than 25 years, Beryl Thompson-McClary's success as a trial attorney can be attributed to three uncommon, dynamic, yet essential features: hard work, a sharp mind, and grit. These characteristics shape her approach to every aspect of life — whether it's being a wife or mother to seven children. She is one of the leading Family Law high net worth cases and criminal attorneys in Central Florida. All it takes is a single meeting to know Beryl Thompson-McClary is a woman of authentic determination to excel and makes it her life mission to make sure others around her achieve their potential too.

Thompson-McClary grew up in Leesburg, Florida, a small agricultural town outside of Orlando, in the midst of the Jim Crow South. She was the youngest daughter of a black business owner in the citrus industry and an insurance agent with one of the first black-owned companies. She learned from her parents that hard work doesn't guarantee success, but it is a necessary requirement to achieve it. And work hard she did. She went on to enroll at the University of Florida on a full-ride scholarship, where she graduated with honors and excelled in intercultural and international relations. Immediately after, she became a JD candidate at the University of Florida, earning her degree as one of the few pioneering black women in the class.

Thompson-McClary has a tough, fighter's spirit, a spirit she brings to each case, ensuring her clients always receive the personalized plan and attention to detail they deserve.

Thompson-McClary spent many years at one of the largest law firms in Orlando, but after the firm's rising reputation of racism, Thompson-McClary felt the need to connect with her clients more deeply and embarked on a journey of her own. She decided to start her own private firm in 1985, where she specializes in complex family, criminal, and probate litigation. Thompson-McClary's track record in her practice has been outstanding. She practices in the federal Middle District of Florida and the Eleventh Circuit Court of Appeals, as well as state and local government. She successfully obtained the release of a prisoner sentenced to life imprisonment at 18 years of age after serving nearly 30 years. She also successfully halted the acquisition and building of an expansion by a hospital corporation over historical roads and properties owned by African American residents.

But it's not all gavels and juries when it comes to Beryl Thompson-McClary. As the wife and career manager of the founder and lead guitarist of The Commodores, Thompson-McClary enjoys attending music festivals, concerts, and shows with her husband. She is also an author. Her new book, *The Next Chapter* (October 2019), was written to encourage people to perform, dream, and believe beyond their expectations and to never let your age deter you from achieving excellence. Recently, Thompson-McClary and her husband Thomas became empty-nesters. When Thompson-McClary isn't advising and fighting for her clients, she's visiting one of her seven adult children in Nashville or New York.

CONNECT With Beryl McClary on Social Media

Website: www.berylmcclary.com

Facebook: www.facebook.com/berylmcclary

Instagram: www.instagram.com/berylmcclary

Twitter: @berylmcclary

Email: info@berylmcclary.com

www.ingramcontent.com/pod-product-compliance
Lightning Source LLC
Chambersburg PA
CBHW070953080526
44587CB00015B/2286